PENGUIN
MASTERING BEHAVIOUR

Payal Anand is an associate professor of organizational behaviour at Indian Institute of Management (IIM) Kozhikode, India. She has been affiliated with IIM Kozhikode since 2019. She has also taught at IIM Raipur and FLAME University, Pune, at various levels. She has been awarded her PhD from IIM Indore. Her research interest mainly includes workplace loneliness, personality traits and emotions. Her work has been appreciated by the international journal of repute such as the *International Journal of Human Resource Management and Journal of Knowledge Management*. She is a recipient of the prestigious 'The Michael Poole Highly Commended Award for the year 2019'.

Celebrating 35 Years of
Penguin Random House India

PRAISE FOR THE BOOK

'Moving into a managerial role for the first time is challenging for most individuals. Congratulations to Payal Anand for providing a conceptually sound yet very practical guide to smoothen this transition. While she identifies the challenges involved, her positive tone should enhance the self-belief and self-confidence of readers. Highly recommended for all first-time managers'

Rishikesha T. Krishnan, *Director and Professor of Strategy, Indian Institute of Management Bangalore*

'Abstracting complexity in wrappers of simplicity is anything but easy, especially when dealing with the human species and their nuances. But Payal has refreshingly handled all this with surprising ease and a lucidity that defines courage. Yes, of course, the ocean of humanity is blue and dark. But wading us slowly instead, through the shallow and still shores, Payal shows us the crystal-clear beauty of the flora and fauna that lies therein in that seemingly opaque vastness that warrants harvest.

Quoting extensively, from Aristotle to Neil deGrasse Tyson, Payal brings home the singular need to understand ourselves and others. Into the stale and hackneyed world of manuals for new managers, Payal introduces an invigorating, read-worthy text that cannot be more handy'

M. S. Suresh, *Chief Technology Officer, Apar Innosys*

'Humans are social beings, and the heavy reliance on each other to survive, thrive and succeed is inevitable. With this backdrop, *Mastering Behaviour: Managing Self and Others* is a practical playbook that should be in the workspace of any young working professional, as it speaks to the pressing behavioural challenges faced by first-time managers and new joiners.

This book provides a wealth of insights related to the power of self-confidence that forges positive relationships, builds resilience, emanates positive aura that gravitates people towards the individual and the priceless gift of feedback—all of which accelerates the transformation into a charismatic leader. The similarities and differences in human nature can be both complementing and supplementing, and hence, the value in embracing a collective-genius mindset is well-articulated.

If you are an aspiring leader, wanting to learn about the blind spots, traps and societal taboos that could cripple your full potential and derail your career aspirations and if you are ready to take the bull by its horns in addressing the root of it than merely addressing its symptoms, this book should be your next must-read.

Professor Payal's indomitable knowledge, interest and keenness to empower the millennial workforce to grasp the mantra of 'self-awareness' to overcome significant personal limitations and reach the pinnacle of their potential shines through these pages'

Raji SenthilKumar, *Global Head of APIs (Application Programming Interfaces) and Access Solutions, Digital Channels and Data Analytics, Standard Chartered Bank*

'I am very happy to note that Professor Payal Anand has written the book *Mastering Behaviour: Managing Self and Others* for working professionals. The book becomes important because as students step into the corporate world and move up the ladder, they have to interact with multiple stakeholders with different expectations and personalities. As a student, success is mostly direct cause and effect; working hard generally results in good grades. However, as working professionals, employees have to quickly move from compete to collaborate mode and learn that interdependence is more important than independence.

The best part of the book is that though this is a very practical, 'solution-oriented' book, yet it has strong conceptual foundation for very typical problems experienced by working professionals. The language is easy to comprehend and solutions easy to implement.

This book, in my opinion, is a must-have for all working professionals, and I am sure it will be soon in the list of bestsellers. I wish her all the best'

Yogesh Misra, *Vice President, Thomas Assessments Pvt. Ltd*
(India and SAARC Region)

Mastering Behaviour: Managing Self and Others is an enjoyable ride into one's world of work. Dr Payal has introduced the real challenges that are ubiquitous yet seldom discussed. For example, Chapter 3 describes workplace loneliness. The author lucidly explains why people experience loneliness and prescribes solutions to deal with it. The book is unique as it is based on empirical data and is grounded in a solid base of research. The book brings out the real professional issues that every manager can relate to. The book drives one to the professional life, illuminates the challenges and provides a new lens through which to look at them. A must-read for practitioners and the academics!'

Sushanta Km Mishra, *Professor, Indian Institute of*
Management Bangalore

'First, I should appreciate the author for her maiden book that illustrates well on how a young manager should be emotionally balanced while executing his or her tasks. The author has brought out various attributes that a low/middle-level manager is subjected to between the workforce he or she commands and the senior management. To conduct daily affairs, personal or professional, we necessarily have to deal with people. For some, the requirements are more by the very nature of the task. For some, this comes naturally, while for others, it's a nightmare. Like in science, so in human science, lesser the friction, smoother the movement. This book addresses the friction points. Every book or product must have a unique selling proposition. This book carries the simplicity of driving home management principles to the unless initiated without burdening them with academic jargon. Some people, especially researchers, scientists, accountants, etc., suddenly get thrown into management world without any formal training and are suddenly at a loss. This book will be a boon for them—holding them by hand while negotiating the 'unfamiliar'. An excellent 'Bible' by Payal Anand and a must-read even for those not involved with low/middle management'

Suresh S., *Scientist 'G'/Additional Director (Retired), CVRDE, DRDO*

'*Mastering Behaviour: Managing Self and Others* is a book that stands out among several other books on a similar theme. The book is a result of extensive research carried out by the author. The best part of the book is that it not only lists the problems faced by first-time managers, but it also offers solution to those problems.

Mastering behaviour is a one-stop solution for preparing oneself for new working circumstances. Payal has brought in an exhaustive perspective on all the behavioural issues that are unavoidable at work. The discussion points are quite pragmatic and relatable, making this book an important read not only for the new managers or managers changing jobs but also for their bosses to familiarize themselves with the possible issues mid-level managers might go through. A brilliant read for academicians and practitioners!'

Kamal Kishore Jain, *Visiting Professor,*
Indian Institute of Management Raipur

Mastering Behaviour

Managing Self and Others

Payal Anand

Series Editor: Debashis Chatterjee

PENGUIN
BUSINESS

An imprint of Penguin Random House

PENGUIN BUSINESS

USA | Canada | UK | Ireland | Australia
New Zealand | India | South Africa | China | Singapore

Penguin Business is part of the Penguin Random House group of companies
whose addresses can be found at global.penguinrandomhouse.com

Published by Penguin Random House India Pvt. Ltd
4th Floor, Capital Tower 1, MG Road,
Gurugram 122 002, Haryana, India

Penguin
Random House
India

First published by Sage Publications India Pvt Ltd 2021
Published in Penguin Business by Penguin Random House India 2023

ISBN 9780143461777

Printed at Replika Press Pvt. Ltd, India

www.penguin.co.in

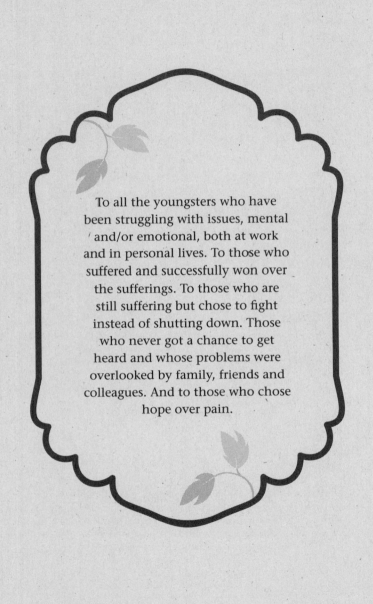

To all the youngsters who have been struggling with issues, mental and/or emotional, both at work and in personal lives. To those who suffered and successfully won over the sufferings. To those who are still suffering but chose to fight instead of shutting down. Those who never got a chance to get heard and whose problems were overlooked by family, friends and colleagues. And to those who chose hope over pain.

CONTENTS

SERIES NOTE

The IIM Kozhikode Series for New Managers has key business and practical insights for management graduates and first-time managers alike. Penned by the distinguished faculty of the premier management institute, IIM Kozhikode, the books in this series are succinct, illustrative and replete with real-life examples. These books will endow new managers with business expertise and empower them as they navigate a volatile and highly competitive corporate world.

NOTE BY SERIES EDITOR

Dear reader,

IIM Kozhikode Series for New Managers brings *Mastering Behaviour: Managing Self and Others* from the esteemed faculty member of IIM Kozhikode—Payal Anand. This book aims to discuss and offer solutions to behavioural and interpersonal issues that new managers face at work.

Behavioural aspects play a quintessential role in a successful career. In fact, as people move up the ladder in hierarchy, the demands of technical skills go down while the behavioural and interpersonal skills go up. In a spread of eight chapters, this book brings about some significant people-related issues new managers encounter at work. Each chapter not just highlights the potential difficulties but also provides remedies to tackle them. The book bases its arguments on three levels. The first level includes the first-hand interviews that the author conducted by doing fieldwork and meeting managers to understand their narratives and some real issues they have been through in their early career, thus providing a pragmatic scenario to the readers, making it more relatable for them. The second level includes arguments based on various secondary research that are relevant to the context of this book. The third level unfolds the arguments based on popular theories from psychology and sociology to discuss problems and solutions based on theoretical groundings.

The chapters are engaging as the arguments and stories are quite relatable and real, thus giving perspectives on some serious concerns that young and first-time managers have at work. Readers will also find the exercises and DIY (do it yourself) sections helpful and interactive. The chapters particularly on managing personality types, stress and loneliness will help the readers get some perspective on these topics essential for leading a better personal and professional life. The collection of interactions shared by the author with her former students who have been working as early managers in their respective places is also engaging to read.

Mastering Behaviour: Managing Self and Others and the other books in the IIM Kozhikode series for New Managers aim to bridge the gap between the demands of the corporate world and quality management education. As a new manager and professional, you will be ready to face the corporate world, and with greater clarity and confidence, after reading the books in this series.

—Debashis Chatterjee
Director
IIM Kozhikode

PREFACE

In my first job as an academician, I was supposed to teach post graduate management students, who probably were the same age as I was and if not, very close to my age. 'Would I be able to do it?' I used to think multiple times a day ever since I had received my offer letter. 'Talk to your colleagues and get some tips'—some of my college mates suggested. Well, though the idea sounded reasonable, the only thing that bothered me was 'what if my colleagues think that I am incapable of performing well at this job'. Thankfully, I realized very soon that everyone is blessed with some strengths and some weaknesses. Why not leverage your strength and hone it, while working on your 'not so strong' points simultaneously?

Having been in the Indian Institute of Management (IIM) system for close to a decade now, documenting my own experiences and those corridor-and-cabin conversations would be sufficient to fill the pages of an entire book. But I wished to take this discussion to an advanced level, where I am able to present the readers some pragmatic issues faced by young and new managers post joining their workplaces. To understand if things have changed with the current generation, I interviewed around 80 ex-students whom I have personally taught. These students either were about to begin work or have been working only for a couple of years. Hence, the chapters in the book are entirely about under-standing some major issues people faced or dealt with, during the initial phase of their career. The first question that I had asked them was pretty straightforward: 'In the beginning of your career, as a young fellow, what problems did you face while dealing with others in your workplace?'

Based on my own experiences and interaction with others, this book offers an outlet to explain why knowing the self and others is important, especially to young working professionals. Using a solution-oriented approach and their applications, this book also offers solutions to new managers as to how to tackle difficult interpersonal situations at work. The book further deliberates and discusses why positive interpersonal exchanges are crucial and what are the deleterious consequences of not being able to make good connections at work. This book is an attempt to provide some practical solutions to difficult issues at work and how one can become better in exploring possibilities in human interactions.

* 1 *

THE TRUTH ABOUT
WORKPLACES

A recent Harvard Business Review[1] article quoted,

> Workplaces are communities build around the
> relationships we have with our peers. When these
> relationships are strong, they can be a source of
> energy, learning, and support. But when they
> fracture, even just temporarily, they become
> sources of frustration that harm both people and
> organizations. Left unchecked, even a small con-
> flict can spiral out of control, leading to anger and
> resentment. That's why managers and employees
> need to be able to manage and rebound from these
> conflicts.

A report[2] established some interesting statistics. It stated
that 85 per cent of the US employees deal with conflict on
some level, out of which 49 per cent is a result of personality and ego clashes. 34 per cent of conflict is caused by
workplace stress.

---

[1] https://hbr.org/2020/02/how-to-mend-a-work-relationship
[2] As stated in https://robynshort.com/2016/02/16/the-cost-of-conflict-
in-the-workplace/#:~:text=85%20percent%20of%20employees%20
deal,conflict%20among%20the%20senior%20team

Wouldn't it be a perfect world if we knew people and their personalities, their preferences, what they are like and their expectations from others? Though this can never be uncovered with unlimited precision, the least that we can do is to start knowing ourselves, be aware of our needs, our strengths and weaknesses. Moreover, knowing others' perspective of us would be the cherry on the top. Once we get an understanding of who we are and how we come across as a person, it becomes easier to empathize with many others and their preferences. However, this isn't as easy as it sounds. If knowing and understanding the self and others were this simple, there would not be very many problems in life.

My recent interaction with the ex-director of marketing at Microsoft strengthens my beliefs about human personality and the way it impacts people. In his words, 'The issue is not just with introverts, it is with extroverts too. An extrovert would prefer to recharge his battery by communicating with others or presenting his ideas to others. At any point in time when he realizes that there is nobody to properly listen to him, it creates some problems. I have been an introvert all my life. I am not somebody who goes out or mingles with people. I have had a handful of people my entire life whom I have called my own. In fact, because of this, I have felt miserable a lot of times. I have lost a lot of friends in personal and professional space. Though I have always tried to reflect upon how and in what context I have lost those people, it has always been a struggle, because I never understood the actual reasons. I could never find out the mistakes I had done. Maybe it's because I could never cope with their energies.'

NERVOUS JITTERS ABOUT WORKPLACE

I recall that on my spouse's first day at his new job (an MBA graduate from IIM), he was feeling miserable already! As he recalls, 'thousands of thoughts were running through my mind—Would the people be nice to me? Would I get like-minded team members? What about my boss? Will he like my working style? Will I make friends at work? Or will it just be like my previous company (he had worked before joining IIM too)?'

My spouse's experience is not exclusive. It is not unusual to have these 'preconceived notions' about the new workplace that bothers the managers-to-be, making them nervous. Transitioning from a comfortable college life to working at an organization can be tricky a lot of times, especially at the beginning of your careers. Young students who eventually become new managers are clueless about the norms, boundaries, roles, new relationships, etc., and hence, make judgements based on their preconceived notions.

As discussed in the Preface, I collected some personal experiences of my former students who are currently part of the workforce. Throughout the chapters, I'll be showcasing little snippets of their experiences.[3] Let's understand from their unique experiences and analyse key takeaways from each life story.

---

[3] The original names have been changed to protect the identity of respondents.

Minisha's story of her first job ever: 'Just like everyone else, I was also very happy after getting first offer from a renowned firm. After MBA, I got an opportunity as a showroom executive in a retail showroom. As a fresher, I had no clue regarding my subordinates' expectations from me as their manager, job expectation from my manager, technological know-how, team management, etc. Basically, I was not aware how to deal with people in a professional environment and no training as such is given in companies on such issues. Clearly, I was unsure of managing four contract staff reporting to me. I am an extrovert, which made my life even more difficult. Getting work done from them was a challenge, as I had become too friendly with them already. Moreover, all of them were technically sound, in fact, better than me. Soon, I realized, even they were not comfortable in reporting to me. To make things worse, my boss was an introvert. Our approaches to issues were different. Well, at least I learned "what not to do in a professional environment". I think I didn't give enough time to understand how organization works. After failing terribly, I learnt the importance of understanding people I was working with.'

What Do We Learn Here?

1. It is very important that both your and others' deficiencies be explicitly discussed. This cannot magically happen. For this, you need to put in efforts in building relationships with your colleagues, subordinates and managers and share things about yourself, instead of being a stranger in team whom nobody knows. Moreover, others should feel comfortable in telling you 'I don't understand what you just said.'

2. Every human being is different; hence, it's important to at least try to understand them and treat them

MASTERING BEHAVIOUR

with respect as a unique individual. It is likely that there will be a personality mismatch between you and your boss and/or teammates. Learn how to leverage it instead of making it a conflicting point.

GETTING INTO A NEW WORKPLACE

Once you join a workplace, a gamut of new challenges comes into the picture. While there are way too many struggles, let me confess that it's a whole new exciting chapter of life. The idea of meeting new people, earning handsome salaries, getting dressed and looking presentable on a daily basis, informal group activities and parties, etc., surely

gives the feeling of butterflies in your tummy. Hence, just like any other life experience, joining a new workplace is filled with mixed emotions. Along with the fun side, there would be a lot of performance pressure (such as closing deals and hitting numbers), exploration of the new territories and genres of work.

However, one thing that's really crucial at a mid-level management is tackling tricky behavioural issues. A mid-level manager, basically, acts as an interface between the top and the low level of hierarchies at work. Naturally, dealing with people day in and day out becomes an integral part of the job. Hence, for a young manager, behavioural challenges weigh much more than technical challenges. You could be sound in technical aspects, but being behaviourally sound is one aspect that will get you success in your new job and will create hurdles if not tackled well.

In the next segment, we shall discuss some important issues that popped up multiple times while talking at length with the new managers. Through the interviews and interactions, it could be derived that the following issues, if taken care of well, may help the work life of a young manager and direct the energy in focusing towards succeeding and moving up the ladder.

CLASHES DUE TO DIFFERENCES IN PERSONALITY TYPES

Disha, one of my ex-students, shares her experience which is also one of the most common issues among working professionals that could be even more crucial for people who just enter a new working environment.

MASTERING BEHAVIOUR

'I was fresh out of college life and I started my career in HR. I was new to the role and to the start-up culture of my company. I am an agreeable person, owing to which, I trust others easily. I also have this constant need to affiliate with others. I started making connections with all 50 employees at this organization. Owing to my personality traits, I had a tough time persuading them to work on assignments. I was afraid, "If I become strict with them, how will I maintain relationships at the workplace?" "What if I hurt them by being rude to them? They will not like me anymore." Obviously, failing to push the team members in order to get work done and, thus, missing deadlines came with its cost. I miserably failed to meet the expectations of my boss and got poor annual review ratings. I had quit the company post that.'

What Do We Learn Here?

While you might have great skill sets, your personality can derail your career right at the get go. Therefore, knowing critical areas of your personality is of utmost importance. What worked in college might not be applicable at work. Pay attention to the lacuna of your personality and try to keep a check on it on a day-to-day basis.

STRUGGLES WITH BUILDING HEALTHY CONNECTIONS AT WORK

One major problem that millennial workforce is currently facing is that of loneliness, both at work and outside. Alongside struggling with being able to connect meaningfully with people, there is a stress of working in a team kind of set-up. Imagine how hard it would be for a young professional to work with a set of people who s/he doesn't connect with, at all. Therefore, addressing such issues proactively is crucial for early managers.

Here is my conversation with another ex-student, Mark:

'My first job got me into one of the most difficult phases of life. While everything else was good, I succumbed to loneliness. During the first few days in Kerala, I was not able to make any friends within the team, since most of them knew each other prior to joining. They were either from the same college or shared a native place. Also, I have felt people who speak the same language are quick in bonding with each other. The culture at the place was different, unknown. I could clearly feel the differences at work. This may have been partly due to regional influence. Transition from college friends' group to being all alone at workplace disturbed me a lot. I was emotionally exhausted due to my loneliness. My main strength and support in those times were my reporting manager and the seniors at work. My reporting manager apparently knew about my loneliness. He used to call me over to his house, or with his family for Christmas celebrations and evening tea and snacks occasionally. That was a ray of positivity and strength in those trying times.'

What Do We Learn Here?

Although loneliness may occur at work, be it your first job or fourth, it has been witnessed that loneliness at work has become quite common, especially in the initial days/months of work. Chronic loneliness can lead to severe physical or mental illnesses. It also deteriorates job performance. Hence, one should take it seriously and seek solutions to overcome it. What is important is to accept it and address it. Either you sulk over it or try to seek self-help, you have to choose. And what you choose decides your fate in the company and in life.

DEALING WITH STRESS AND EXHAUSTION

One thing that my interviewees stressed on, over and over, is tackling extreme stress and exhaustion both emotional and physical in the new job. The sad truth is that stress cannot be avoided at work, especially for rookies. Stress is bound to happen.

In the words of Gopi,

'I think college days are like watching a cricket match from the stands. We create our own worlds where our friends occupy the seats around us. We do not concern ourselves with much and just enjoy the play of life. But moving into the phase of work and career, things slowly get complicated if we are not willing to learn and adapt. It now suddenly is like playing in the ground. A sudden transition, we are bound by certain rules. This, in itself, was a challenge for me, to adapt. More challenges followed. Being a project manager, every work was time bound. Even though there are time schedules, a lot of time tasks are required to be completed in an urgent manner. This was the toughest thing for me. I am somebody who finds comfort in fixed schedules. Uncertainties stress me out so much that I am at my worst in terms of both performance and overall behaviour. Eventually, I started making mistakes, avoided talking to people and became a loner. This created a constant fear of rejection in me. I even started feeling that my boss was conspiring against me.

This was five years ago. Much later, I realized that it was my fault, not my boss'.'

What Do We Learn Here?

Stress incapacitates true human capabilities and hinders the performance. Moreover, it colour blinds us from seeing the realities. We may start believing in things that may not be always true. And that would let us to prejudge people. Seeing everyone with an open mind is tough, but it is an important quality that needs to be developed in life. Therefore, understand what troubles you the most at work and elsewhere and work on it. Recognizing and addressing the stressor is really important.

STRUGGLING TO UNDERSTAND PEERS AND THEIR ORIENTATIONS

While it is important to understand your own personality and that of others, it's equally important to understand your colleagues', their working styles, their life orientations, etc., to be able to fit well in that job and that working environment. My ex-student Saurabh, who works as an early manager with one of the biggest automobile companies in the country, mentioned:

'There is a huge gap between my expectations and the reality. Work life is different, and it took time to understand it. It requires getting things done through collective negotiation and bargaining. I used to voice my concern to the senior management assertively as I thought that my company is ethical and value driven. Argument with the senior employees is much better than others, and welfare activities are an ongoing, time-consuming process did not convince me much. Being rather aggressive, I shot off a letter to the senior management, after which my suggestion was accepted and put into practice. However, this did not go well with my immediate seniors, and things did not go well for me. My outspokenness and brashness as a young trainee put me in a spot of bother on many occasions.'

What Do We Learn Here?

One thing important to note here is not everybody is meant for every job. There needs to be a person–organization fit, otherwise it becomes quite difficult to coexist, for both the parties. At times, such issues lead to severe conflicts that might later become unresolvable. In case there is no person–organization fit, one must first understand the paradigm in which one is working. This gives an idea of whether to be diplomatic in approaching certain issues. Wherever possible, one should avoid ruffling feathers and be patient at early stage of careers.

POOR CONFIDENCE AND SELF-DOUBT

Another issue among new managers that's quite pervasive is the feeling of 'self-doubt', that they are 'not ready yet'.

Here is Sumant's story.

'I had started my career with XXX Brands as the assistant restaurant manager. While I loved what I did there, I must confess, I faced some major issues during early career years. One of the most stressful aspects of starting a new job is having to catch up with the information being passed on as quickly as possible, leading to information overload, especially for a fresher. We had a completely packed three-day orientation programme, and by the end of third day, we had tons of information to store and process. I was handed over a file which had a detailed four-month training programme and a 500-page book, which I had to memorize for my upcoming evaluation. That stressed me out like crazy because I was not expecting this, at all. This led to a lot of confusion. I was not even sure whether I was capable of handling it or not. I was doubting myself constantly. I feel that support from colleagues in the early days makes a lot of difference and creates a lasting impression about the organization. During my initial days, I met a few individuals who would not help me nor answer my questions/queries. Instead, they would delegate their work and throw tantrums about not allowing for breaks, not signing on my training plan, not planning a week off in the roster or making last-minute changes in roster, etc. This led to another major problem, that is, the ice was never broken with colleagues or superiors; I hesitated to ask questions. That contributed to an incomplete training process. Ideally, the manager should make the freshers feel welcomed, introduce to the team and make him/her comfortable. He/she must empower the fresher to ask as many questions as he/she can, to get a quick understanding of the work. It is the responsibility of a manager to help you boost your confidence, be there to solve your queries and guide you during the start of the career. As the first-time manager, I found it difficult to transition from a colleague to a superior, all the while maintaining positive personal relationships and gaining respect. I was at my lowest self-efficacy during that period. Though I totally loved my job, these are certain things that still make me feel bad about my initial days of career.'

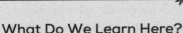

What Do We Learn Here?

There are some important aspects to be noted. Youngsters quite commonly doubt themselves and their capabilities in the beginning of their career. No doubt, during such challenging shift from one phase of life to another, your confidence is tainted or threatened. However, note that your confidence in your abilities is one of the significant factors that help you succeed at work. Moreover, it is okay to be confused, feel ambiguous about the roles and responsibilities and, hence, seek support of peers. While, at this juncture of your career, it is crucial to have a manager who is a great supporter and mentor, not all of you will be lucky enough to find such managers crossing your path. Remember that *people leave managers, not companies*.

KNOWING THE HALF TRUTH ABOUT SELF

The whole idea is to have better self-awareness, so that new managers may have an opportunity to improve themselves and work on areas that can probably interrupt the career success in the long term. While a lot of us know about our strengths and weaknesses, that's not sufficient, as we do not have complete information about the self. There is a portion of the self that's noticed and observed by others, something that your colleagues might know but you don't.

As Pinki narrated,

'Being a fresher, I was clueless about my company's processes and expectations. I was introduced to the team which had already a set of experienced people with different age groups and mindsets. I was expected to match their level and catch up to them at work. Since I was from an IIM, I was given a tough client. New work culture can, at times, be frustrating, especially getting to know your teammates. Teams shape common interests, trust and allies. Lack of trust and transparency are the two major issues

I faced at work. Lack of transparency is becoming the presumed norm in project and programme management, and expectations are growing. Trust is crucial to teamwork, and it starts with people knowing each other. You need to be acquainted, both professionally and personally, particularly in projects where tensions run high at some point. Otherwise, team members will not understand each other, they won't want to engage with each other because they haven't made that human connection, and they won't fully trust each other. For me, it took time to gain the trust of my teammates to get them on board with my ideas. Thankfully, I understood early that before proposing any idea to the table, we must ask for the feedback and suggestions of teammates. We must build the reputation of being clear-headed, objective and reasonable. We must be flexible in incorporating others' ideas and suggestions. While I did make many mistakes, I admitted them and apologized instead of trying to cover them up. That surely helped. Indeed, my teammates' poor work habits affected my performance. I made sure I explained to them humbly and respectfully how their behaviour is affecting me and what changes can help me. I made sure to understand the common interests, team goals and tried building trust within the team and attempted to prove my mettle. Engaging in team-building activities, too, helped me get to know my co-workers. I think, as a fresher, everyone goes through this. Today, as a leader, I have always ensured a right ambience for rookies, so that they can easily mingle with the team and create the cohesiveness.'

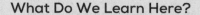

What Do We Learn Here?

One thing that's crucial for your success is to understand that your performance in a team depends upon how early you settle in a new organization and team, by adapting to the culture and new people. Mingling with your new teammates requires you to build trust, which takes time. Moreover, how you come across as a person impacts your relationships with peers and juniors. While self-awareness is important, as it allows you a chance to work on your critical areas, ensure you seek corrective feedback periodically from your team members.

NOT A CAKEWALK, FOR SURE!

What are some of the thoughts running through your mind after reading these stories? Were you surprised to read them? While some of you reading this book are maybe freshers or have worked prior to joining your MBA, either way, I am sure these stories have reminded you of some people you have encountered in your lives including yourself. These issues do not exclusively pertain to workplace, but they are just much more prominent at work than elsewhere. Now, do not get me wrong. With these stories, I am not trying to discourage or disappoint you in anyway. I am not saying workplaces are horrible and you are only going to suffer. I am NOT saying that at all!

But the idea of the book is noticeably clear now. We will look at some typical problems young managers go through at work that hamper not just their performance but also their psychological and emotional well-being. I am sure for the first six months, during your *honeymoon period at work*, you are going to have your own share of fun. The issues start once you delve deeper into the given roles, and that's when your interdependency on your colleagues start creating hiccups in your path. Hence, through this book, we will learn how to tackle or address those issues pre-emptively to avoid such situations. Apart from this, we will explore some techniques, using which we can handle such troublesome events at work.

SOME COMMONALITIES IN THE LIFE STORIES

One thing that we found common in all the life stories of these MBA graduates is that all of them mentioned some specific challenges pertaining to human behaviour, either their own or others'.

Believe me, I only asked them a simple question, that is, 'one challenge that you faced as a fresher in your workplace?'

I'm not surprised that all of them discussed behavioural issues as the main challenges. This does throw some light on the fact that as we move up the ladder in our organization, the requirement of technical skills goes down and behavioural skills goes up. So, at a mid-to-top-level management of any company, around 80 per cent of the skill sets required to successfully perform any job are human and social skills. Moreover, being an MBA graduate, it is apparent that you would be working as an interface between the top and bottom of the organizational hierarchy. It goes without saying, you cannot manage it without understanding people. And to accomplish this, the first step, which mostly goes unnoticed and is super underrated, is to manage the self. Understanding the self will allow you to gain perspective on your acts, keep it in check and enable you to sort out interpersonal issues in the best possible way.

I am sure some of you wonder whether is it really your fault every time. Well, it doesn't matter, because what's most important is the outcome. In this case, the outcome is your sanity, satisfaction, well-being, relationships and performance at work. Ultimately, all of us want to survive, prosper, cherish, belong and become, don't we? Hence, it's best not to debate whose problem it is or who is at fault. We must ensure to create a healthy work environment for ourselves and for that of others by diminishing the effects of our negative behaviour, accepting others with their flaws and exploring the possible opportunities in developing mutual relationships. And what's better way than to start with ourselves?

* 2 *

UNDERSTANDING YOUR PERSONALITY

An email in my inbox that I received from a female student, ambitious and willing to make a name for herself in the corporate world, awaited my response. She was only two months old in the IIM system at that time and was expected to sit for the internship placements soon. Here's how it read:

'I'm an emotionally stable person, but here, within one month at IIM, I feel like giving up; I have had breakdowns many a times and after you mentioned about neuroticism in today's session, I started crying. In my previous job before joining college, this happened in the first month of my work, but the intensity was lower than the current scenario. I am not able to manage time properly. I don't even get time for myself. Moreover, I am unable to understand courses and assignments. I get demotivated and feel like not continuing here. Thankfully, I spoke to one of my batchmates, and he is helping with academics. Still, due to the continuous demand of time, it gets difficult for anyone to give me some time.'

As a professor, this is not the first time I have received an email like this. I have had several such endless conversations, at times, direct one-on-one discussions or corridor talks and, other times, via emails, texts and pings, with youngsters regarding their issues of being confused about their personality, not being able to cope with the stress and pressure, facing unmanageable situations, in fact, to the extent that many of them wanted to quit in the first few months. What pains me the most is that they do not know what exactly is causing them to think or behave in such a manner. Many of us are tempted to make an armchair diagnosis without understanding the real issue. At times, it helps the sufferer, other times, it makes them feel worse and life gets hard without guidance to address the grassroots issues. Fortunately, the problem is not as grave as it appears to be to the young people, who are on the verge of starting new careers but struggling with issues of managing self. I am not saying that self-management is an easy task. I am stressing that one can grow to learn to manage behavioural issues. Knowing certain nuances about oneself can help a great deal.

So, first things first, ask yourself how good you have been in leading yourself in the past. And if you think you are self-aware already, my next question to you is—how aware are you of yourself to know if you are self-aware? In simple words, are you self-aware enough? Confused, right? Let me share another email from another young mind that I received right after she dropped her papers in her first job.

MASTERING BEHAVIOUR

'I need your advice on something very personal. Even though I have a decent profile (neither so stellar nor so poor), I feel like I'm good for nothing or fit for nothing. I know what I'm doing is overthinking and exaggerating trivial issues or a small backlog. This is reflecting in my career quite a lot. I don't know if anyone would believe this. I'm not even speaking or putting forward my thoughts in office discussions, thinking that, whatever I'm going to say won't be of any use or value. I've been in silent mode since I started sensing this problem. In short, my problem is I'm aware of what my problem is but not aware of the solutions or action plan to rescue myself from this before it's too late.'

Though this young lady claimed to be self-aware, the chances are she knows little less than what she thinks she knows of herself. She needs to know that she is a unique human as all of us are, having some fantastic traits that can work in our favour, if dealt with and managed properly.

So why self-awareness is crucial, especially for a new manager, and what is required by us to be fully self-aware?

While you may have peers, who happen to be your friends or have bosses who are super supportive, one thing that you cannot do without is knowing yourself fully. Because while other factors are external and are subject to change, the only factor that will be your constant is yourself. That's why knowing yourself inside out becomes important. As a young manager, it's not unusual to have shaky confidence or self-doubt. You might also have some traits such as being short-tempered or too talkative. But self-awareness balances out every other undesirable aspect of yourself. If you are aware of what can go wrong because of these traits that you possess, you will behave cautiously and carefully. Hence, self-awareness gives us power to influence life outcomes to some extent.

Leading oneself is about taking charge of your anchors. It is about personal leadership. It is the ability to define a direction for your professional and personal life and move in that direction with consistency and clarity. Leading the self indicates taking responsibility to understand what drives your behaviour, attitudes, perceptions and emotions. It is about knowing yourself—what you want, your strengths and weaknesses, and how others perceive you. Note that it's okay to have traits that we might not be very proud of. All of us are unique somehow, and when I say unique, I include both good and bad qualities. However, what is more important is to understand these two crucial aspects in this regard:

- *Self-awareness*: Self-awareness is knowing our strengths and flaws. It is an essential step towards personal leadership. This makes it possible for us to accept ourselves and identify areas for personal development.

- *Self-management*: Leading the self also includes self-management, or the ability to control one's emotions and behaviours to achieve our objectives. Understanding how we react to events and respond to others help us change our behaviour if habits limit our effectiveness.

THE INFAMOUS BIG FIVE PERSONALITY FRAMEWORK

The first step towards self-awareness is knowing who you are. Understanding your personality—the right areas and the critical ones—to a great extent, solves issues surrounding your concept of knowing oneself better. Personality can be understood as relatively stable patterns of your attitudes or behaviours. The whole of knowing oneself can be comprehensively conveyed using the infamous Big Five. According to personality framework, our personality traits can be divided into five sub-traits. This will be discussed in the next section, but before that, let me ask how your ideal job looks like? Do not overthink now. Do not say anything 'manageable' (I know the desperation of getting into any job in the beginning of the career!). Well, my ideal job involves sitting in a quiet office amidst the nature, working on solo projects and, once in a while, bumping into my colleagues near the kiosk to get that feel of social life at work. That does not mean I am boring or that I hate people; in fact, I like social interactions, but to a certain limit. I still go to informal office gatherings and chitchat with my colleagues and their families with full enthusiasm, but I like to finally settle in a corner with colleagues who also happen to be my close friends.

Did you guess who I am? Am I an extrovert or an introvert or neither? Yes, I am selectively social. The idea is to make you understand that interpreting behaviours of others and self is not as easy as it sounds. In fact, I would go ahead by saying that this is probably one of the most complex things to decode. Though we often judge people on the basis of what 'we see' on the surface, the reality is what you see of a person may or may not be their personality. That's why we need to dig deeper a little bit further to understand what personality really means.

The Big Five model defines human personality types as follows:

- *Openness to experience*: Curious, adventurous, flexible, artistic, imaginative, a wide range of interests, willing to pursue many things simultaneously are some of the most common traits possessed by people high on this dimension. A low on openness to trait indicates close-mindedness, not willing to explore or adventure, prefer to be in a rut, seek structure, work in a well-defined system and prefer doing one thing at a time.

- *Conscientiousness*: If you are disciplined, focused, hardworking, organized, methodic, unrelenting, responsible, meticulous and detailed, you are high on conscientiousness. People around you think of you as dependable, given the amount of effort you put in and the sincerity with which you do the given tasks. If you are low on conscientiousness, you might be unorganized, not so detailed, laid back or procrastinate sometimes and do not go the extra mile while performing the tasks allotted. You might not be systematic or pay too much attention to details.

- *Extroversion*: You got this one right! Extroversion, the most used personality label, is inclined towards being talkative, social, gregarious, assertive, having a vast network of people, energetic and outgoing. If you are an extrovert, you like being the centre of attraction, don't you? (people around you might think of you being attention-seeking, but does it matter to you?). You can be easily found near canteens, coffee machines, or places that are usually crowded. Maybe you like to wear clothes that are bright and catchy. As an extrovert, you may want to be everywhere (otherwise, have a feeling of FOMO—fear of missing out). Low on extroversion or, as is popularly known, introversion indicates being self-content, aloof or like being with limited set of people, reflective, silent and like fetching energy from within.

- *Agreeableness*: Kind-hearted, sympathetic, cooperative, concerned for others and generous are some qualities that define you if you are high on agreeableness. People around you like you much and trust you. You might get perturbed by others' issues and care about their problems a lot of times. If you are low on this trait, you might like to not indulge in others' issues, be disagreeable without getting bothered, not be concerned about them a lot of time or let others' problems take away your peace. To convince you, others need to bring you some logic. You might not be hesitant when it comes to refusing others' ideas or proposals.

- *Neuroticism/emotional instability (or, the opposite, emotional instability)*: Neuroticism, or emotional instability, involves moodiness. High on neuroticism indicates you are someone who experiences a lot of stress, worries a lot, gets upset easily, gets easily overwhelmed, gets instigated by small triggers, short-tempered or discontent about many things. Low neuroticism indicates high emotional stability. Emotional stability means being calm, relaxed, composed, not disturbed easily and able to tackle stressors; in fact, you do not stress yourself out. You would maintain your calm even if I told you that the building's roof would fall on you! Relatable much, eh?

So, in short, consider the below-mentioned dimensions of your personality.

Low		High
Aversion to the new experience	Low to High on Big Five Personality Dimensions	Openness to experience
Careless		Conscientiousness
Introversion		Extroversion
Disagreeableness		Agreeableness
Neuroticism/ emotional instability		Emotional stability

SOME MYTHS!

- Introverts are less confident or unhappy people.
- Extroverts are always happy.
- Agreeableness is equivalent to being a yes-man.
- Conscientious people have no personal life.
- Neuroticism is a personality disorder.

CAN THERE BE A DOWNSIDE TO MY PERSONALITY TYPE?

Yes! The extreme of anything is bad. Though each personality type is blessed with some great qualities, it comes with

Extrovert

Introvert

its cons. The next section describes what could be a possible characteristic to each personality trait that might hinder your day-to-day life, disturb others with your mere presence and derail your career if not managed well. While it is great to understand your good and bad qualities, I suggest you take it with a pinch of salt. Do not get overwhelmed and become too harsh on yourself. Do not try to change yourself to become someone you are not.

So, let us first understand the good things about your personality type. Refer to the tabulated format for a snapshot of things that can work in your favour if your personality is managed well (Table 2.1).

Well Well ...

Does everything look hunky dory? But wait, I haven't yet come to the bad side. The next segment (Table 2.2) will help you understand the negative or the grey areas of your personality type.

Note that just like every coin has two sides, your personality has two different aspects too, that is, the good and the ugly. In Table 2.1, we have already discussed about the good side of your personality type. The next segment discusses in brief about some of the critical areas that can work as a hindrance in your life, say in your career success or progression, your relationships with others, your friendships, your intimate relationships, your participation in the groups, or work teams and so on. Let's understand some of the issues that needs to be managed well for each personality dimension.

Introspect and see what from Table 2.2 looks familiar to you. It is imperative to note that, at times, you might not

Table 2.1: Strength of Each Dimension

	If High	If Low
Openness to experience	An explorer; ready for new challenges; no stress under unforeseen circumstances; can go without planning; excited about new things or learnings; manage well with non-routine tasks; do not seek standardizations in things	Works the best with standard kind of work; follows the rules and do not question them much; no anxiety about regular or routine work; can manage well with monotonous tasks as well; do not seek newness in things
Conscientiousness	A perfectionist; serious and sincere about the work assigned; need no external push to finish the tasks on time; believes in work first, play later; complete tasks with full focus and flawlessly; drives others to work with perfection	A regular next-door guy; do not push others much for work; keeps low expectation from others in terms of tasks; chilled out attitude; play first, work later; keep the work environment cool and easy; relaxed and stress-free attitude
Extroversion	Look cheerful and happy; talkative, hence, help others in removing boredom; social; break ice for others; make others at ease by initiating the conversations; full of energy; keep the aura of their surroundings vibrant	Self-content; reflective and thoughtful; calm and poised; never steal others' moments; silent observers; maintain an environment of peace and silence

(Continued)

(Continued)

	If High	If Low
Agreeableness	Come across as a positive person; blessed with empathy; sympathetic; provide others space to share their experiences or issues; approachable; warm hearted	Do not poke in others' lives; do not hesitate in calling spade a spade; upfront about the issues; not interested in issues of others; give others their required space; rational in their arguments or conversations; straightforward
Neuroticism	Create sense of urgency in groups; believe in planning out things beforehand; do not wait for the last minute to complete tasks; Nudge others for the due reminders; do not hold back their expressions; easily predictable	Stable in their emotions; do not get overwhelmed easily; assume the world is a happy place; optimistic and hopeful; do not express their negative (or positive) emotions; maintain a calm environment at work or elsewhere

Source: The author.

Table 2.2: Critical Issues of Each Dimension

	If High	If Low
Openness to experience	Constant desire to do something different; urges to seek new experiences; take too much on the plate; not being able to work in a standard or routine environment; constant bouts for creativity	Difficulty in brining creativity to the table; demotivation with frequent changes in work; difficulty in starting things from the scratch; need guidelines or blueprint to perform tasks
Conscientiousness	At times, over critical; too much expectation from others; trying to be a perfectionist, even during time constraints; get too lost in smaller details that lose out on the bigger picture; might come across as strict, stringent or tough; others might put additional work on you; uptight	Not bother much about the smaller details of the task; focus is to finish the task; might compromise on task quality; others might not depend or rely; might come across as laid back or careless; might seem unsuitable for serious or critical tasks

(Continued)

	If High	If Low
Extroversion	Too talkative at times; have poor listening skills; seem dominant to others; might come across as arrogant or full of self; too much energy might intimidate others; attention-seeking; constantly feel the need to bring out ideas; seek their energy from outside always; can get easily demotivated if not given a chance to speak; have fear of missing out	Get exhausted with too much talk; might feel out of place a lot of times; constantly need their own corners; come across as serious; facial expressions are limited; voice modulation is limited; get exhausted in social gatherings; might come across as reserved or self-centred
Agreeableness	Easily get occupied and overwhelmed with others' issues; gullible; inability to say no to others; make decisions emotionally; get hurt easily; need people around them who can understand them; difficulty in taking decisions rationally; overthink about others' issues; tend to make others' issues their own	Difficulty in thinking emotionally; rationality might blind from using or understanding emotions; might come across as self-centred; might seem rude to others; difficulty in understanding others' issues a lot of times

| Neuroticism | Easily get overwhelmed; often stressed with small triggers; might upset or disturb others with their negative emotions; frequent mood swings; get tensed when planning goes wrong; inability to perform under extreme pressure; might get nervous easily; can easily succumb to physiological issues | At times, too calm or poised; no sense of urgency; difficulty in pushing the team through tight deadlines; might come across as unaffected or indifferent about the issue; might be in their own la-la land; do not quite anticipate or foresee real problems |

Source: The author.

notice your behaviour bothering others. It is absolutely normal. What is considered wrong is to know about it and still choose to ignore it instead of fixing it. Note that the idea is to become the best version of yourself. If you know what can make you a better person, then why not go ahead and work on the improvement areas? Do not we all like people who come across as balanced instead of annoying or weird? Then let us start from today. Notice every big and small behaviour of yourself and ask yourself, 'Could it be because I am too conscientious or because I am too agreeable?' You know yourself the best. If the answer is yes, then choose the path of remedial actions. You will definitely like yourself much more, I promise. In Table 2.3 are some remedies or suggestions that will take you a long way in making a better version of yourself. Pick and choose one thing at a time, instead of bombarding yourself with loads of change at once. Take baby steps.

Can I Say My Personality Type Is Meant Only for Certain Kind of Tasks and Can Incapacitate Me from Doing Other Kinds of Work?

To answer this question, let us do a small experiment.

Take a pen and paper and write your full name (not in caps though) with your preferred or dominant hand. Now, switch the pen to the non-dominant hand and do the task again. I am sure you made some observations. Can you think of a few things you just noted? I am confident I am not wrong while I say this:

1. It took more time to record with a non-dominant hand.

Table 2.3: Suggestion for Improvement on the Critical Areas of Each Dimension

	High	Low
Openness to experience	Evaluating risk before you start something new; control your urges for creativity; set goals and try sticking to it; prioritize your goals, see what is more important; make trade-offs; let go of unimportant things; learn to be more practical; start following a daily routine in at least some aspects; plan ahead and stick to it	Figure out new genres to experiment; do not hesitate in experimenting; step out of the comfort zone; set target for something new every month and stick to it; increase frequency of exploring new things as you become comfortable slowly; do not stay with only one activity for long, try to alter it
Conscientiousness	Trust your co-workers; delegate work to them without doubting, you may give detailed guidelines in the beginning if it bothers you much; encourage co-workers/team members to bring in new ideas; do not micromanage; be accommodating and accepting; set time duration for various activities and stick to it; set agendas with each and every task and stick to it, not all the tasks require you to be a perfectionist	Assign a devil's advocate for feedback on your work; set reminders to finish work on time; understand the demands and quality standards of projects or tasks and stick to it; be receptive to feedbacks; remind yourself to be sincere about the assigned tasks

(Continued)

	High	Low
Extroversion	Improve listening skills, make sure you pay full attention to the speaker instead of thinking what to say next; nod and show you are involved in the conversation; stop speaking after every four sentences; offer others to speak and to pitch in their ideas; try monitoring your energy, notice when it can become annoying to others	Indulge in more social activities, start with initial few; try to participate in various group activities with variety of people; keep a mug or a friend who constantly reminds you to frown less, smile more; work on your facial muscles, ease them out; figure out your hobbies and join such groups of like-minded people
Agreeableness	Learn to say no, start with family and friends and then practise on acquaintances; think rationally about the pros and cons of a situation; accept that not everyone is equally important; set clear and definite boundaries; let others fight their own battles, you are not needed everywhere; do not be submissive, be assertive when required	Try building a rapport with your cohorts; crack jokes on yourself to make others feel comfortable around you; tell more about yourself to others, preferably the vulnerable part of you; be self-deprecating in front of others to make them feel at ease; give rationale to your decisions; be more receptive to feedback; be supportive to others' viewpoints

| Neuroticism | Curb your expressions, especially in formal set-up; plan things ahead and stick to them; respond, do not react; do not respond to emails immediately that bother you or put you in discomfort; do not respond in conversations where you feel angry or anxious; do not reveal your vulnerable side to every person, they might take undue advantage; seek therapy, counselling or help of psychologist, if something bothers you constantly; maintain a journal every time something disturbed you and find patterns and work on them; indulge in yoga, meditation, physical exercises to release happy hormones; indulge in activities that are engaging and keep you calm; vent out in whichever way possible in an informal set-up; accept that you have temper issues and consciously act on it | Try to be more accepting of others, even if you do not understand their emotions; be supportive; use statements such as 'I understand', 'It is okay to feel this way', 'I know someone else who has gone through the same', 'I have been through tough situations too', 'it will be fine with time', etc.; try expressing yourself bit by bit; appreciate others, give them gifts or handwritten notes; make your loved ones feel important and assure them that you understand them; watch out your tone, it should not sound rude; be more polite |

2. It might have taken you much more time to write your name with a non-dominant hand, as compared to the dominant one.

3. It would have put you in discomfort. There is a sense of familiarity with your preferred hand, which is why, when you use the other hand, you went beyond your comfort zone to write your name and, hence, the discomfort.

4. You were extra cautious and observant of your hand-writing.

5. You might not be happy with the kind of output that you see with the non-dominant hand. That means your overall performance is affected.

Unless you are ambidextrous, you will not be able to perform this exercise with ease. Okay, the takeaway is not that you can (and should) never write with your non-dominant hand. This exercise explains that if you use your non-preferred or non-dominant hand, you would still be able to write but not to your satisfaction, and you might not be exhilarated with the overall performance.

Your personality is exactly like your dominant and non-dominant hand. Some traits are dominant in nature, that is, an extrovert likes to be an extrovert unless forced to be silent, not socialize, etc. Being extrovert is just the dominant personality type. Suppose you are put in a situation where you are all alone, there are no social circles, nobody who is there to listen to you or hang out with you. You will feel demotivated, right? You will feel demotivated to an extent that you would want to look out for groups where you can belong, seek out more friends, might also want to change your jobs in extreme circumstances.

Having said that, it does not mean if you are put in a situation that demands you to be an introvert, or a situation that does not fulfil your requirements as an extrovert (social circles, engagement activities, belonging groups, lot of talks, opportunity to speak, etc.), you will fail to perform. You would still be able to perform or stay in that job, however, with a lot more discomfort and with added pressure. And that is why I emphasize that every time you choose a job for yourself, you must take care of a few things; for example, is there a person–job fit? Is that a 'person–organization' fit? Understand the demands of the job and whether it is matching with your personality type or not. That matters a lot. The reason being, if you are put into situations that do not support your personality type, there are remarkably high chances of you being dissatisfied, disengaged at work, and we definitely don't want that. We want a job that makes us happy. A job that makes you believe in the value you are creating. Your job should not discourage you from starting your day on a happy note.

Moreover, a personality fit is not the only challenge your job is going to throw at you. There are various reasons that can dissuade you from enjoying your job. While you cannot manage the non-controllable factors, you can and should at least take charge of things that you can control.

Is There Any Sure Shot Way of Knowing My Personality Type?

Yes, take the infamous Big Five personality psychometric assessment (Refer to the appendix given at the end of the chapter).

What if I Do Not Like My Personality?

Note the following points:

- Personality is not synonymous with behaviour. How you behave is an outcome of the interaction between your personality and the situational forces. Thus, do not take it on face value.
- All traits have its pros and cons. Extroverts are impulsive. Agreeable individuals are easily influenced. Conscientious individuals are uptight. And the list is long.
- If you have options, find an organization that suits you. Look for a person–organization and person–job fit. Not all organizational cultures or jobs are designed to suit everyone.

PERSONALITY IS MORE IMPORTANT THAN YOU THINK!

After having delineated the Big Five personality dimensions, I think you got at least some takeaways. Not that you do not know already who you are as a person. The intention behind discussing your personality is to point out what are some of the best qualities in you and a few aspects that are not so helpful that can be worked upon.

1. You must have observed some colleagues are too talkative, some are too silent. Some of them are too controlling, some are just too gullible. Accept that all of us have some discrepant areas that require improvement. Take that positively, and refer all the tables wherein I have offered significant suggestions for you. Try to incorporate those suggestions or

MASTERING BEHAVIOUR

remedies on a day-to-day basis in your workplace and see if there is a positive impact of it on your personal and professional life. I bet; you will feel much better about yourself if you comply to the suggestions made in this chapter based on the issues highlighted.

2. As a young manager, you will juggle between various roles and responsibilities. To be successful, you need peers to help and support you. The idea here is not just to understand your own personality but also to accept your peers with their flaws. So now you know, while, for example, you could be high on conscientiousness and your expectations on the quality of a project or a work is pretty high, not everybody's like you. There could be a possibility that you end up working with team members who are not high on conscientiousness, which means the small details that you would like to see and fix those nitty gritty elements might create difficulty for others. They might not be able to cope with your expectation of perfectionism. While this was just one example (of conscientiousness), there are a number of examples to explain how different people are different and that could create clashes in their expectations or in terms of having a good relationship.

Well, yes, there will be conflicts and there will be mismatch of expectations. There might be scenarios where your thoughts would not be in sync with others and vice versa. You have to deal with it. Now that you know, in detail, how different people are different, try being more self-aware and accepting than you are currently. You will see it working magically in improving the relationships with your colleagues.

Q: I wish to share that I face a lot of difficulties making friends at work, or otherwise, and mingling with people. I am scared to take the first step to start a conversation. In my current job, I could make only two friends. I have gotten a lot of hate, and my colleagues make perceptions that I am an arrogant and rude person who thinks very highly of herself and does not want to talk to them. But it is not true. To my close circle (the two to three friends that I could gather in my life till now), I come across as an immensely helpful, emotionally sound and a receptive person. I do not know how to change that perception of my colleagues towards me, because it bothers me a lot. I sympathize with them, but I am afraid to talk to them, maybe because of the past experiences I have had in my life. I have faced high emotional stress due to this reason.

A: Though we all have needs to belong or socialize as humans, it varies and is subjective. In your case, your needs are sufficiently being met by one or two friends, which is fine. You need not push yourself to make more friends at work if the existing ones sufficiently fulfil your needs and requirements of interpersonal relationship. Besides, you have relatives, family members, etc., that must be counted as your circle too. So not just core, the peripheral relationships are also very much part of your life. But note that what's more important is having a collegial relationship with your colleagues. That should be your real concern. Make sure you share things about yourself once in a while, such as who you are, your likes, dislikes, your hobbies, etc., so that your colleagues get to know you better.

Yes, individuals like you might come across as reserved or self-centred. But do act upon it only when you feel it is important. You should not be over-critical about yourself. Extroverts are no less criticized; they are criticized by their counterparts for being too vocal, assertive, poor listeners, trying to catch attention of others constantly and so on. So, let me say, it is not others who should be blamed. They will judge you for whoever you are. You need to accept yourself fully and not let their judgement affect too much. Work on managing your emotions and try not having perceptions about 'what will they think of you'. Do not let such issues bother you much. If it disturbs you a lot, just vent it out (talking or writing, whatever makes you feel better, do so).

Q: **Can neuroticism happen when we cater to a new situation or work? In general, I am an emotionally stable person, but within one month in my new job at XXX, I feel like giving up; a lot of times I have even had breakdown, and in fact, I start crying sometimes, for no reason. Previously, it happened in the first month of my work (job before undergraduation), but the intensity was lower than the current scenario. My concern is, is it happening because of the current situation and spikes in work? Because I am not able to manage time properly. I do not even get time for myself. Moreover, I am unable to understand**

the assigned activities. I get demotivated and feel like not continuing here. Thankfully, I spoke to one of my peers and he is helping with work, but due to the continuous demand of time, it gets difficult for anyone to make some time. My scores are: extroversion: 3.5, agreeableness: 4.1, conscientiousness: 3.4, emotional stability: 2.7 and openness to experience: 2.8.

A: Note that under extremely stressful circumstances, people tend to behave just the opposite of their true nature. If you feel you have been an emotionally stable person earlier and post your joining of XXX, the issues have started occurring, it could very well be because of the situation.

Your low score on openness to experience is playing the role as well. You seem to be a person who likes to work in a familiar environment, most of the times. The current environment is new and unfamiliar to you. But once you settle in with the new culture, you might not face it anymore. Time management is one of the most common issues in the beginning of any work. Talk with your seniors/superiors. I am sure they have stories to tell. Many of your seniors have gone through similar issues; things become fine in three to six months. So, do not panic. If it gets overwhelming, always talk to peers, seniors and seek suggestions.

Q: I took all the personality tests (Myers–Briggs Type Indicator [MBTI], Big Five, etc.). I also love to know how other people have performed in it. In future, when I need to make decisions which impact how people perform or when teams are to be built, how do I avoid falling in the trap of making an armchair diagnosis and letting my own biases affect these decisions and the people who I work with?

A: It is a mistake people often make.

First of all, accept that you do not know everything; hence, it is okay to take a step back rather than making an armchair diagnosis. Take decisions objectively; it helps a great deal. In workplaces, as a manager, it is possible to objectively assess behaviours or personality types of people using assessment questionnaires. Besides, you may learn techniques of observation and probing. Do not hesitate in learning more about varied cultures and backgrounds of others. Since you already keep an interest in this area, it will never bore you. I also suggest read some good books that offer you perspectives that are tried and tested. They will impact your decision-making skills in the long run.

Q: I have taken Big Five personality tests, and what I found striking is that most of my scores are between 3.3 to 3.7, but extraversion is low, and now in XXX, being a fresher from a not-so-fancy school and college, I sometimes find it intimidating to mingle with people. In small groups, I am the funniest person you will find, and when I am tasked with something, I do it very professionally, but lately, I have been stressing a lot on how I fit in, in these new surroundings.

A: Do not see being low on extroversion as a challenge. Though we all have needs to belong or socialize as humans, it varies and is subjective from person to person. In your case, your needs are sufficiently being met by small group of people, which is fine. You need not push yourself to come across as an extrovert.

Try taking baby steps. Try talking about yourself in front of others, given a chance. Share your narrative, your stories, your past experiences. This helps others to know you better. Humans are curious by nature, and they do not pay much heed once they have got enough information about you. Your new job will throw many more challenges at you, which all extroverts might not be able to handle. Let your time come; keep honing the skills you are good at. Simultaneously, learn things that you would like to learn and can be useful in terms of helping your peers (helping them with tasks, entertaining them with your creativity, or any small thing). You are an emotionally stable person; that is going to help you in a great way during your job. Plus, you have an advantage over others as you can switch and adjust yourself in situations smoothly (while many others might struggle with it).

As extroversion comes across as quite a bold personality type, we tend to get confused about it and give too much weightage to it thinking it is a favourable personality type. Do not confuse yourself with that bias. Be fully confident about who you are and accept yourself; that is what matters the most.

APPENDIX

A BIG FIVE PERSONALITY ASSESSMENT

Your scores will range from very low to very high.

Steps to assess yourself on Big Five personality scores (Table A.1):

1. Do not take the test under stressful condition. You might get biased results.
2. Fill up 20 questions on your personality by marking yourself from strongly disagree to strongly agree. Do not overthink. Mark based on what comes to your mind first when you read the question. No score is a good or bad score.
3. Now, calculate your final scores for each dimension and take an average. Your scores on each dimension should remain between 1 and 7.

How Do I Interpret My Scores?

For all the dimension, the more towards 1, the lower you are on that dimension, and more towards 7 indicates being higher on that dimension. To get an accurate idea of your scores, you may follow:

1–3.24   : Very Low

3.25–3.99 : Low

4–5.49   : Average

5.50–6.24 : High

6.25–7   : Very high

Table A.1: The Short-form Big Five Questionnaire[1]

Generally or typically, I …	Strongly Disagree	Disagree	Slightly Disagree	Neutral	Slightly Agree	Agree	Strongly Agree
1. Am the life of the party	①	②	③	④	⑤	⑥	⑦
2. Sympathize with others' feelings	①	②	③	④	⑤	⑥	⑦
3. Get tasks done right away	①	②	③	④	⑤	⑥	⑦
4. Have frequent mood swings	①	②	③	④	⑤	⑥	⑦
5. Have a vivid imagination	①	②	③	④	⑤	⑥	⑦
6. Talk a lot	①	②	③	④	⑤	⑥	⑦
7. Am interested in other people's problems	①	②	③	④	⑤	⑥	⑦
8. Often put things back in their proper place	①	②	③	④	⑤	⑥	⑦
9. Am stressed most of the time	①	②	③	④	⑤	⑥	⑦
10. Am interested in abstract ideas	①	②	③	④	⑤	⑥	⑦

[1] M. B. Donnellan, F. L. Oswald, B. M. Baird, and R. E. Lucas, 'The Mini-IPIP Scales: Tiny-yet-effective Measures of the Big Five Factors of Personality,' *Psychological Assessment 18*, no. 2 (2006): 192.

11. Talk to a lot of different people at parties	①	②	③	④	⑤	⑥	⑦
12. Feel others' emotions	①	②	③	④	⑤	⑥	⑦
13. Like order (or things being arranged)	①	②	③	④	⑤	⑥	⑦
14. Get upset easily	①	②	③	④	⑤	⑥	⑦
15. Do not have difficulty understanding abstract ideas	①	②	③	④	⑤	⑥	⑦
16. Like attention from others	①	②	③	④	⑤	⑥	⑦
17. Am interested in others	①	②	③	④	⑤	⑥	⑦
18. Keep things organized	①	②	③	④	⑤	⑥	⑦
19. Often feel gloomy	①	②	③	④	⑤	⑥	⑦
20. Have a good imagination	①	②	③	④	⑤	⑥	⑦

Table A.2: Final Scoring

Personality Dimension					Total	Final Score = Total/4
Extroversion	Q1	Q6	Q11	Q16		
Your scores						
Agreeableness	Q2	Q7	Q12	Q17		
Your scores						
Conscientiousness	Q3	Q8	Q13	Q18		
Your scores						
Emotional instability/Neurotic	Q4	Q9	Q14	Q19		
Your scores						
Openness to experience	Q5	Q10	Q15	Q20		
Your scores						

Source: The author.

I Am an Average Scorer! How to Interpret My Scores?

If your scores are more towards the average of the continuum, you are an adaptable person, quite accommodating and may easily switch to the demands of the situation without complaining much. While these are some good qualities about you, you are not refrained from having some critical areas. You might be unable to make quick decision, follow majority a lot of times, be in dilemma and/or a state of conundrum when it comes to choosing a side or take a stand. Others might perceive you as someone who is manipulative, have no stance of your own,[2] unprincipled or calculating. If you do not want to be in situations like these, make sure to explain your stance to others, follow objective criterion, past trends to make decisions, or follow the footsteps of the experienced ones. Clarify others about your choices and rationale behind your preferred (or not preferred) choice.

---

[2] https://httpsreview.mit.edu/article/how-to-become-a-better-leader/

* 3 *

AVOIDING
WORKPLACE LONELINESS

According to some recent studies[1] on loneliness at work, the loneliness scores for Gen Z and millennials in 2019 accounted for 49.9 and 47.7 per cent of the total, respectively. That means almost half of the young population at work, or even more, comprising mostly of newcomers and early career executives, feels lonely. Loneliness hampers productivity, lessens engagement and commitment with the work and organization. Loneliness is as common as the common flu.

Loneliness happens when you feel there is no meaningful connection in your life despite having many people around you. In simple words, you are not happy and satisfied with your social connections. Isn't it bewildering to find that one of the reasons of stress and anxiety during COVID–19 times is subjective social isolation aka loneliness? More than three in five Americans are lonely, with people reporting feeling left out, poorly understood and lacking companionship,

---

[1] https://www.forbes.com/sites/nextavenue/2020/02/25/whos-lonely-at-work-and-why/?sh=af6984370379https://www.cigna.com/about-us/newsroom/studies-and-reports/combatting-loneliness/ https://www.cigna.com/about-us/newsroom/studies-and-reports/combatting-loneliness/

according to a recent survey.[2] The UK and Japan have ministers for loneliness 'to tackle the sad reality of modern life', as reported by a magazine article.

India is not far behind in loneliness. In a 2020 survey, the likelihood of being lonely has gone up to as high as 50 per cent. That means that half of the sample population in India may be feeling lonely. Loneliness in Indian young adults is becoming a serious concern in the country. The suicide rate per 100,000 population in 2016 was 16.5, while the global average was 10.5 per 100,000.[3] One of the main reasons for increasing suicide, as cited by the World Health Organization, remains loneliness. The most vulnerable to loneliness is the 15–29-year-old. That indicates that youth in the country are at the most risk of loneliness. Just imagine, India is one of the youngest countries with more than 54 per cent of the total population below 25 years of age and is prone to loneliness. This is an alarming sign, to say the least.

The increasing rate of loneliness, depression and suicide is not surprising anymore. Young working professionals, especially the newcomers, struggle with many issues that potentially can make them lonely and, in turn, lead them to depression. In their personal lives, youth of today is becoming a victim to loneliness due to their lifestyle, being too dependent emotionally on parents or others, lack of self-awareness, excessive social media usage and

---

[2] https://www.npr.org/sections/health-shots/2020/01/23/798676465/most-americans-are-lonely-and-our-workplace-culture-may-not-be-helping

[3] https://www.who.int/india/health-topics/suicide

MASTERING BEHAVIOUR

its negative impact, confused about life in general, trying to create impact, feeling miserable when met with failures and so on.

In professional life, factors such as being part of an unnecessary competition, constant race to win, constant comparisons and trying to maintain equity, trying to find shortcuts to success, inability to withstand failures at work, trying to change things that are beyond control, being ambiguous about role and career, generational differences, etc., potentially lead to loneliness. I am not saying that we are always responsible for our loneliness. Several environmental factors such as COVID–19 can impact your state of loneliness, too. However, if we proactively work on ourselves to avoid loneliness, understand the potential environmental factors that can make us lonely and be aware of the self and surroundings, it will help us a great deal in eluding the detrimental experience of loneliness.

Loneliness is entirely subjective in nature. For some of us, as few as one or two people would suffice the definition of 'meaningful social connections', while even 10 is too small a number for some others. That is why what X interprets of his/her experience of loneliness might be different from Y's. But one thing remains consistent: loneliness is an extremely intense negative emotion and is harmful to our mental, emotional and physical state.

LONELINESS AT WORK

While there is much research and talk on loneliness, the exploration of loneliness at the *workplace* has been abysmally low. It is quite recently that the importance of loneliness at the workplace has garnered some attention. The investigations on workplace loneliness have started flourishing in the past couple of years. Loneliness is pervasive. That means people can be lonely at all levels, across hierarchies, contrary to much popular belief that *loneliness happens only at the top*.

I have spent years in grounding my exploration of loneliness in personal and professional space. Given the severity of the issue and considering the rising number of suicides due to professional reasons, I started exploring loneliness in the workplace context during my doctoral education. During my explorations of workplace loneliness, I did fieldwork at multiple levels. To understand its nitty-gritty elements, I first began interviewing working professionals to understand its existence at work. Most of them, if not all, have at least once suffered with moderate to chronic levels of loneliness. I was baffled to know their experiences of loneliness (it was kind of scary in some cases) and how they had fought it. Some of them could not deal with it properly, which caused them chronic health issues.

SOME FINDINGS AND TRUTHS ABOUT WORKPLACE LONELINESS

I explored workplace loneliness in two different phases. In Phase 1, I had conducted 30 qualitative interviews with working professionals to understand their experiences (as mentioned earlier) and interpretation of their reality of loneliness. In Phase 2, I conducted a survey-based (self-reported) study on around 1,300 professionals, out of which 700 were newcomers, to capture their perceptions about self. The aim of the research was to understand real life experiences and possible factors that might impact the experience of workplace loneliness. In the context of organizations, loneliness is agreed to be a predominant workplace emotion and has the potential to affect both the employees and the organizations.

During the interviews, I found some intriguing facts. I found important factors affecting workplace loneliness. Some crucial factors leading to workplace loneliness, which emerged from my analysis of the interviews, include 'lack of meaningful connections at work, low confidence in one's ability to deal with adversities, value incongruence (both with colleagues and employer), lack of meaning and value in the work one is doing, lack of avenues to socialize beyond work and too much politics'. Note that while some factors leading to loneliness can be controlled, others cannot. For example, you cannot do much about an organization that does not provide you much scope for interaction beyond work or is too political in nature. In this chapter, I will discuss some common reasons for loneliness among youngsters in personal and professional spaces and a few pragmatic solutions to alleviate it.

WHY LONELINESS HAPPENS AT WORK AND OUTSIDE

An ex-student wrote to me after four months of joining his 'dream' company:

As an entry-level employee, my manager is everything for me in my job. But whenever I approach my boss, I find him praising another guy. He praises their little work and never recognizes my great work. These are the moments when I feel marginalized and feel bad for myself. I often feel sad and pity myself. This feeling has eventually created a distance between me and my colleagues and made me lonely.

And another one working in a large automobile company mentioned:

Because I am a shy person, I feel I am not competent enough to generalize my thoughts or express adequately with my colleagues. For example, due to my shy nature, I shrink at times, and that shrinkage causes me to remain with my thoughts. If am not going to express, I will not be able to form good relationships. I remain with my feelings. And, therefore, I feel lonely a lot of times.

In a recent article published in *MIT Technology Review*,[4] it has been claimed that neuroscientists are exploring the cause of loneliness through neurotransmitters. While biological sciences are investigating loneliness for an explanation, parallel fields have given structure to the area by explaining why people feel lonely in the first place.

This has been delineated by the famous British Psychologist John Bowlby, notable for his contribution to attachment

---

[4] https://www.technologyreview.com/2020/09/04/1008008/neuro science-loneliness-pandemic-covid-neurons-brain/

MASTERING BEHAVIOUR

theory.[5] He explains that like kids, adults also have some need for intimate relationships or a confidant. This need for close attachment or confidant dramatically influences the quality of life and social engagements. According to Bowlby, not just the kids but even adults search for attachment figures in their lives. For example, it is school friends who become an essential part of our lives during our adolescence. As we grow older and hit adulthood, our spouse and kids become the source of gratification. The need to attach (and belong) is so ingrained in human beings that we always seek the 'attachment figure' at various life stages. At workplace, we constantly seek to build relations, be part of the groups, etc. For new joiners or even new managers, this need is even more strong as they step into an unfamiliar environment altogether. Note that a sense of attachment with colleagues gives us a feeling of safety, warmth, security and fulfils our emotional needs at work. Hence, we strive to spend our time with those who satisfy such requirements. Unfulfilled needs (failure in finding close or meaningful relationships) and breaking attachments with loved ones are the causes of our loneliness.

STIGMA AROUND LONELINESS AT WORK

In my first job, I recall my conversations with a young colleague, who was always afraid of being judged by others. He would constantly text me to take him along with me for breakfast and lunch, as we used to eat in the office canteen. I vividly remember him telling me, 'I have hopped from one group (informal) of peers to another, but I could not

---

[5] John Bowlby, *A Secure Base: Clinical Applications of Attachment Theory*, vol. 393 (Milton: Taylor & Francis, 2005).

feel connected with any group. I have been trying for the past one year to find a group of people I can stick with, but I feel I failed miserably. But no matter what, I do not want to be seen alone. I am afraid of sitting alone at the lunch table. So, please accompany me if it is not too much to ask.'

Being his colleague, I felt it is my responsibility to help him. I had all my sympathies with him. I would try to sync my timings with his as much as I could. But it was not doable or manageable always. There were days when he would go alone. I would reach late and spot him sitting in a corner, avoiding eye contact with others, assuming nobody will see him (and judge). Then he would wait for half an hour or so for me to finish my food to accompany him to the office block. He wanted *to be seen* with somebody. He was not doing this for himself. He was doing this for others. Most of his energy was consumed in portraying himself as a 'sociable' chap and 'having colleagues who are also friends' to others, while the reality was stark different. I know it is so sad to even think about it. I know how miserable he would have felt with each passing day. This made me wonder why I would give so much weightage to the thought 'what others think of me?' I understood it quite late that it was not his fault. He was forced to behave in this manner. He was conditioned to the idea that a sociable person is the one who is well fitted in the society and is accepted by others. Unfortunately, being seen alone is a sign of weakness. Walking alone or eating alone or sitting in the office cafe and snacking all by yourself invites judgements from peers.

Worst thing here is, there is so much stigma attached to the loneliness that people are afraid to seek help. The constant fear such as 'What if everybody in my peer group gets to know I am not part of any group?' 'How shameful it is that I do not have any colleagues who are my friends?' 'What if they think it's a mental disease I am suffering from?' resists people from looking out for help.

For decades, researchers have talked about the societal taboo attached to loneliness. Well, how will we put that literature to use if people still have that fear of being judged? To understand if workplace loneliness is still stigmatized, I conducted a small experiment a few years ago. I was addressing a group of working professionals belonging to mid-to-top level in the hierarchy in an auditorium. While talking about life in general, I asked, 'How many of you feel lonely at work?' Not a single person raised their hand. Having been in this field for many years now, I knew that people are probably hoarding the truth, may be out of fear of being judged by their colleagues. Right after the workshop ended, I handed a two-page questionnaire to the same audience which assesses their personality and loneliness. Of course, people were truthful in this assessment as it was kept confidential. Once the assessment was complete, it was shocking to see that around 10 out of 30 were suffering with chronic loneliness.

It is so unfortunate that in current times, on one side when we are celebrating our freedom, freedom of thoughts and speech, on the other side, we are still caged inside with such shallow thoughts and fears. We cannot really blame the sufferer. It's the society as a whole that has created such taboo around mental health that every time it sees a person being deviant from 'normal', it quickly pigeonholes them as 'crazy' or 'bonkers'.

The fact that everybody goes through the experience of loneliness speaks volumes about its pervasiveness. If loneliness is so common, why do we feel so much of shame about feeling lonely in the first place? Do we feel 'embarrassed' when we catch a flu? Do we 'hide' it from others when we get a headache? Do we feel like a 'loser' when we get a stomach ache? Sounds awkward, doesn't it? Why would we even feel bad about a headache or a stomach ache? I am sure you must be thinking this right now. Why is loneliness treated differently then? What makes it different from other issues? That it is a negative emotional experience or that it pertains to your mental health? What is it, after all?

This issue is equally conspicuous in workplaces. Even in progressing times like these, workplaces witness stigma around loneliness. The stigma is so widespread that employees carry work mask and pretend everything to be fine. Needless to say, it is killing you under that mask with each passing day. In fact, acting superficially leads to more cognitive and emotional dissonance. Why is loneliness stigmatized in workplaces? There are two essential aspects to ponder in this regard, that is, evolution of stigma around loneliness and self-stigma of loneliness.

THE STIGMA AROUND WORKPLACE LONELINESS IS SOCIALLY CONSTRUED

Everything that seems deviant from the definition of 'normal' has been stigmatized, be it loneliness, HIV or leprosy, for that matter. So, what is 'normal' is *socially construed*. Society, at large, decides what is acceptable and what is not. Individuals who fit in with the socially constructed definitions of being normal are the ones who are accepted by people in society. And why is that? We tend to stereotype and, therefore, discriminate those who seem different from us.

Anything that looks different or alienated is counted as 'idiosyncratic'. Since a lot of people at work tend to be in informal groups, that has become the 'normal' way of living. Anybody who doesn't appear to be part of informal work groups or sits alone at the café seem abnormal. Recall, we have always questioned the kid who does not have friends in the colony. Unless we understand the root cause of a particular behavioural manifestation, how would we reach to the root cause of the problem and alleviate it? Remember how Sheldon's parents (in the series *Big Bang Theory* and *Young Sheldon*) felt embarrassed in society because Sheldon did not have friends or he did not 'fit in'? The fact was that Sheldon did not really 'need' many friends, all the time, to accompany him. Is this socially accepted? Clearly, not. In Sheldon's case, it did not bother 'what others thought of him' (a bit extreme). But that's not the reality. In reality, it bothers us so much. It impacts out conscious and subconscious thoughts.

In office, employees who are subjectively isolated or lonely are looked down upon. They are the 'centre of all jokes'. They are always judged, rumoured and made fun of. The idea is that if you are not seen around people or look disconnected or disengaged from others, you are labelled as 'nuts'. Your loneliness is seen as a 'personality issue'. You are judged as 'arrogant', 'unfriendly', 'unsociable', 'somebody lacking social skills' or 'aloof'.

MASTERING BEHAVIOUR

WE ARE SELF-CRITICAL AND TOO JUDGEMENTAL ABOUT OUR EXPERIENCE OF LONELINESS

A young manager at an infamous international bank told me once, 'It's been two years. None of my colleagues is my friend. I think I am dysfunctional in some way.'

Thanks to constant judgements and social conditioning, we blame ourselves for not feeling connected with peers or not having enough friends at work. When we feel lonely, we take the blame on ourselves. 'I must be unattractive', 'I am the odd one out', 'nobody wants to be friends with me', 'I am not part of any social group while everyone else around me is' are some of the harsh judgements we make for ourselves. We conclude that there is some fault in us for feeling this way. Though we feel horrible about the entire experience of feeling disconnected, we tend to hide or suppress our feelings.

For early managers, self-critical behaviour is quite damaging. Self-doubt has a spillover on various other work aspects such lower task performance, dissatisfaction with the team, feeling of quitting the workplace or just being a dormant or indifferent employee of the company. Do not feel you are lonely because you are unpopular. You are lonely because your vibes do not match with others around you. It has nothing to do with you having a certain personality.

SO, WHAT IS IT THAT WE FEAR?

Why are we so afraid and ashamed of admitting that we are going through an experience of negative emotion, that is, loneliness? The constant conditioning that 'being alone is bad' has created the fear of being rejected and ostracized. Since loneliness has been seen in such bad light for so many decades, it is natural for lonely individuals to feel embarrassed. For so long, we were taught to behave in an appropriate manner and be liked by others. Thus, we want to be likable; that is socially desirable behaviour. For so long, we were taught to be in groups (i.e., how sapiens evolved). Thus, we want to be accepted and be part of the groups. We fall into the trap of 'fitting in with the norms of society'. And, therefore, once loneliness creeps in, instead of fixing it and nipping it in the bud, we start hiding it with a perpetual fear of being judged by others. This becomes a vicious cycle, leading to chronic loneliness, depression and what not.

DO NOT CONVINCE YOURSELF THAT 'IT IS OKAY TO BE LONELY AT WORK'

When we feel lonely, we tend to justify the state by thinking loneliness teaches us independence and makes us do things on our own. At work, you must have heard people saying, 'It is okay. Anyway, I am not here to make friends.' That is where we are wrong. Do not confuse loneliness with aloneness or solitude. You did not choose loneliness. Loneliness does not lead to positive life outcomes, whatsoever. Loneliness, thus, is not favourable to your survival. The thought that 'loneliness can be good for me' should be reappraised as loneliness in any manner is not favourable. It impacts your brain, mind, physiology and genetics and makes you weak.

Suppose you are suffering from acute loneliness; you can do certain things to fix it (discussed in the latter part of this chapter). It is worrisome, but things are still under control. It can be fixed or mended. However, if you suffer from prolonged loneliness, you need immediate help from a psychologist/ mental health expert. Do not shy away from seeking help. Due to the stigma attached to loneliness, there is a lack of awareness among the population. We do not know how to manage our loneliness. We do not know when it becomes life-threatening (chronic loneliness leads to depression and suicidal tendencies, at times forcing us to end our lives).

WHY WORKPLACE LONELINESS IS BAD?

As workplaces are heavily dependent on interpersonal exchange relationships and people spend more time at work than at home, relationship in the workplace is crucial for the employees. However, it is becoming more difficult for employees to establish meaningful workplace relationships leading to loneliness.

The bad outcomes of workplace loneliness are not hidden anymore. Workplace loneliness is distressing. It impacts how employees think and behave. It impacts their emotions. For example, loneliness creates a feeling of hopelessness and senselessness. It makes people negative to everything around them, be it people or objects. As a result, loneliness further leads to detachment and withdrawal from people and work. Moreover, it is contagious, just like any other negative emotions. Hence, workplace loneliness not just impacts the lonely employee, it also impacts their co-workers. Research has found that workplace loneliness increases job burnout, hampers creativity and performance on the job, makes people leave their companies including other adverse consequences.[6]

LONELINESS AT WORK: HOW TO PREVENT IT?

As mentioned earlier, when we seek solutions to fix it pre-emptively, we need to remember that some things are beyond our control and might not have answers. If it cannot be repaired, it is better to get rid of such situations that are impacting you emotionally, mentally or physically. I have mentioned a few methods below that can help you avoid loneliness in the first place. Consider them as the best practices in life that can keep you away from it.

ESTABLISH MEANINGFUL SOCIAL CONNECTIONS AND DEVELOP SECURE BASES

We have established sufficiently, in this chapter, the importance of meaningful connections. I think I need not reiterate its importance. What is significant to understand here is that it takes time to establish meaningful social circles, especially when you are new to workplace. Meaningful connections or relationships indicate the social affiliations that you consider valuable and worthwhile. For example, you might be waiving to your colleagues daily as soon as your reach the office. But can you count all those colleagues in your list of meaningful affiliations at work?

---

[6] See: P. Anand, and S. K. Mishra, 'Linking Core Self-evaluation and Emotional Exhaustion with Workplace Loneliness: Does High LMX Make the Consequence Worse?,' *The International Journal of Human Resource Management*, (2019): 1–26, https://doi.org/10.1080/095851 92.2019.1570308.

Of course not. Do you share a space with them to talk about what you feel about your boss or that other colleague who always comments on your confidence or looks? Probably not. Therefore, these are just co-workers. You might have an amicable relationship with them, but they cannot be counted as your meaningful work connections. There must be handful of people whom you can call your 'own', people who would listen to you and understand your feelings. People you can share your feelings with without thinking twice. They are your meaningful connections. And we all need such positive attachments and affiliations in our workplaces to feel secure, safe and confident. These people are our secure bases, who help us manage our negative emotions by being present for us when we need them.

Loneliness is prevalent among newcomers and veterans, both. It is more difficult to establish meaningful connections in the workplace than in personal life. At work, the risks are higher, especially when we are new. It takes around 8–12 months to socialize with norms, cultures, expectations, roles and workplace climate. It takes time to understand who the like-minded ones are and if they have space for you in their cliques. Hence, it is natural to feel acute levels of loneliness once you join a new place. The best thing to do is to not panic and to not start hating the workplace or yourself. Give it some time.

SHOW MATURITY IN UNDERSTANDING YOUR COLLEAGUES' POINTS OF VIEW

We, humans, tend to judge others too quickly. That's how we have evolved. However, there are errors and biases we make while judging others. Have you ever noticed we remember insults more than praises? It is easy for you to recall a colleague who made remarks on your hair or appearance six months ago. We remember bad experiences with others more than the good ones.

Adverse events and information attract us more than positive ones. Our brain catches negative information from the surroundings much faster. This definitely affects our cognition, attitude and behaviour. We tend to see more negatives in others than their positives. This is commonly known as negative bias. We are quick to get instigated by negative stimuli in our environment. This is definitely a huge reason we get quickly disappointed in others, hurt easily, lose trust in others and dwell on negative thoughts about them. This vastly affects our relationships with colleagues. In fact, studies say, we meet more negative interpersonal encounters at work than positive.

While it is not always the case that you are wrong, many times there is a possibility that you got hooked to negative information about your colleagues or work in general. There is a good chance that you felt disappointed in the minuscule of unimportant remarks by them (that ideally should have been brushed under the carpet), felt crushed, humiliated, or cheated and lost trust in them. In fact, this phenomenon works on a loop, meaning the more you react to a negative stimulus, the more you get disappointed and anticipate more disappointment in the future. Due to a lack of trust and dissatisfaction, we perceive our colleagues negatively and make adverse decisions. This is harmful and has severe negative consequences, including loneliness.

Next time, if your colleague passes a negative comment on you, reappraise the situation by justifying why they would have said so. Maybe they had a bad day or is frustrated with something. Perhaps what they said is accurate (you looked shabby or underdressed, and this person is quite upfront in speaking their heart out). Reappraise the situation with a more positive approach. Tell yourself, 'you are too new in the workplace to judge others'. Or 'this person is too emotional and over-expressive about certain things'. Listen to it, forget and move on rather than thinking about it the whole night and feeling miserable about it.

LOWER DOWN YOUR EXPECTATIONS FROM COLLEAGUES

In most of my interviews with lonely employees, one common denominator that comes out is 'people are too selfish out there'. To be frank, if you expect everyone around you to be honest, selfless and trustworthy, you are living in a fairy-tale land. First, what is right or wrong for you might not be the same for your colleagues. Do not take it personally. Humans have evolved to act selfish, prioritize themselves and their needs and maximize their resources over others'. That has been delineated under the discussion on 'survival of the fittest'. In the book *The Descent of Man*,[7] Charles Darwin mentioned, 'He who was ready to sacrifice his life, as many a savage has been, rather than betray his comrades, would often leave no offspring to inherit his noble nature.' Darwin considered altruism as a fatal challenge to natural selection.

Two things are clear—people calculate risks and rewards in every social exchange, even if it is an intimate relationship

---

[7] https://en.wikipedia.org/wiki/Reciprocal_altruism_in_humans

with a spouse and there is the act of selflessness that is accepted and appreciated in the history of evolution. If that is the case, how can we expect others to be altruistic, exchanging niceties and pleasantries all the time?

Hence, having too high of an expectation from your colleagues seems unjustified. Cut some slack there. Either avoid them or cut ties if it bothers you too much. Sooner or later, you will find peers who are like-minded. Until then, be patient and understand why 'acts of selflessness' don't exist.

HAVE AN INTERNAL LOCUS OF CONTROL AND BELIEVE YOU CAN MANAGE THROUGH THICK AND THIN BY YOURSELF

In the words of one of my interviewees, a counsellor and senior HR working professional in the apparel industry: 'If you are inherently weak and if your locus of control is external, you have a high dependency for mental support from the outside world. You will need these anchors (people) to latch on to or lean on emotionally, which is why feelings come in. If you are inherently strong, you deal with it in your own ways. You do not need others. And I have seen both the extremes of it. Happiness lies in the external world is a myth. And once you realize that your happiness lies in you, then you are absolutely okay. There is no question of unhappiness, depression or loneliness.' In my empirical investigation, it came out that individuals with an external locus of control are more prone to being lonely, personally and professionally. Locus of control indicates to what extent you feel you have control over events that influence their life. For example, you could be a person who thinks no matter how hard you try, in the end, the person who is lucky will get promoted to the next level (external locus) or the one who believes 'I deserve this position as I have worked hard for it. I will get it' (internal locus). Internal locus reflects high degrees of self-esteem and self-worth. People with an internal locus of control are not affected by others' opinions and thoughts adversely. They do not care much about 'what will others say?' In fact, there is a slew of research that has established that internal locus of control leads to a satisfaction at work and in life. On the contrary, external locus of control leads to low satisfaction, disappointment in oneself and at work. Such people tend to be unhealthier and suffer more with feelings of loneliness, hopelessness or alienation.

To summarize, if you are the one who attributes the cause of events to the outside world, credit success or failures on external factors or circumstances, does not believe in self-capabilities, you are more prone to loneliness than your counterparts with an internal locus of control. Try shifting your focus internally more than externally. Start taking charge of your good and bad deeds. Believe in yourself. You have immense power to make things happen. Start taking control of your life decisions. Accept criticisms from others but do not depend on others for your life events. Once you start owning your ups and downs, successes and failures, you will become more accepting of yourself. You will feel more satisfied with life. Even if you failed, you would have all the reasons to explain to yourself why you failed.

Note that too much of the internal locus of control can be equally harmful. It can blind you and make you too self-absorbed. Hence, while shifting yourself from external to internal locus of control, be flexible and accept constructive criticisms or suggestions from colleagues or superiors. This will help you balance out the risks of a high internal locus of control, if at all.

LONELINESS AT WORK: HOW TO DEAL WITH IT?

In the previous segment, we understood things that can help us avoid workplace loneliness. However, it is not always possible to escape loneliness at work. Truth be told, loneliness will hit you at least once. While the preventions help you proactively work on escaping workplace loneliness, learning how to deal with it will help you deal with situations wherein loneliness has already crept in. The following suggestions, if followed seriously, can help you control loneliness at an early stage.

CHANNELIZING NEGATIVE EXPERIENCE INTO POSITIVE

Despite being aware of the importance of preventing loneliness, at times, things go out of our hands. At times, situations in the workplace play a much more vital role than you had imagined. Afterall, you are a novice, and you might have not faced such hurdles earlier. In such situations, you might feel alienated or estranged from the colleagues or workplace. Despite having secure bases at work, you might feel no one stood by you. It is not their fault. You are new to the place after all. No one wants to take a lot of risk and support a newbie.

There are two ways to deal with this situation. One, you sulk everyday about it. You feel tired and disinterested before even heading to work. Or you attend office with least energy and dilly dally with your deadlines. Your work is getting majorly affected and so is your life. The other way of dealing with this situation is to understand the situation and accept your state of being lonely at work. You might feel that things are going wrong in your first job ever and, on the top of that, there seems to be no scope of substantial relationships at your workplace. That also indicates you have more time in hand as you are not indulging much in corridor talks, gossips and longer landline phone calls with colleagues across workstations. Why not utilize the feeling of negative emotions in opportunities to explore opportunities at work? Channelize your intense emotions in making yourself more productive.

I suggest you utilize this extra time in either focusing fully on your work and increasing productivity or start exploring other projects/activities wherein you can contribute.

MOVE AWAY FROM SELF-CRITICISM AND ACCEPT YOUR SELF-STIGMA

It is often seen that lonely people are full of self-doubts and self-deprecation, thanks to the social conditioning. This is especially prominent across first-time managers. Newbies at work suffer impostor syndrome (chronic self-doubts and feelings of inadequacies[8]) much more than veterans. Hence, it is obvious that loneliness is credited more to self-criticism than anything else. For example, 'I must be a bad colleague that is why I am lonely' or 'I am not competent enough. Therefore, nobody likes to talk to me'. To be in

---

[8] https://hbr.org/2008/05/overcoming-imposter-syndrome

self-doubts and feeling ashamed of oneself is adding to the stigma around loneliness. That is the reason many people are not comfortable talking about loneliness.

However, if you really want to help yourself and others, it is better to speak about your experience of loneliness to your colleagues or superior instead of hiding it. The only way to win over that stigma is by talking about it. Choose people who will take out time for you from their busy schedules to understand and listen to your issues. You should also cognitively offload it by not just speaking about it but also sharing your experiences with others by writing about it. You may use that space on internal blog of your company, or write an article on your experience in the company magazine.

There may be many other young managers like you who must be going through the same; you never know! It is important to understand that until we talk about our issues openly and accept them confidently, no one else will.

DO NOT HESITATE IN ESTABLISHING NEW CONNECTIONS

Most of the times, we socialize only with the project team that we belong to. As it is, newcomers do not have many avenues to build connections outside work. New roles and responsibilities, ambiguities, long working hours, socialization with the organization, etc., takes away most of the day.

Moreover, it has been witnessed in the past that lonely people lack trust in their social circles and, hence, shy away from making any further social connections. They emotionally distance themselves from team members and

MASTERING BEHAVIOUR

fear getting into new relationships. Lonely individuals are often attracted more towards negative information about people, events, situation, job, etc., and tend to feel negative about them. This continues on a feedback loop and never allows one to come out of loneliness. That is how acute loneliness converts into chronic loneliness a lot of time.

Do not be averse to establishing new connections just because your past experiences with colleagues were not good. In a romantic relationship, if you have had a heart-break once, will you simply assume all prospect partners to be untrustworthy? Not really. Why should you punish yourself and others for someone else's mistakes? So, be flex-ible, explore your opportunities to build more connections beyond your team. Join new groups, clubs, committees, strike conversations, express yourself, listen to them and hang out with like-minded people. They need not be neces-sarily from your team or department.

CONSULT A MENTAL-HEALTH EXPERT

Seek out help without hesitating a bit. Do not postpone it assuming it will be fine on its own. No! It does not fix on its own. In fact, loneliness, if not dealt properly, leads to severe consequences. Apart from the consequences such as poor performance and disengagement from work, loneli-ness at work dampens creativity, increases intention to leave the organization and, most importantly, it brings down the cohesiveness among the members in a group.[9] Hence, in every way possible, loneliness can possibly hamper your

---

[9] https://www.tandfonline.com/doi/full/10.1080/09585192.2019.15 70308

job outcomes. As a young, fresh employee, you do not want to take risks.

So, take it seriously. If it does not help you, move on to an expert. Seek therapies. If you genuinely want to come out of it, you will. No one can stop you, not even your loneliness.

I have discussed both proactive and reactive steps to tackle loneliness in this chapter. So, next time if you are surrounded by colleagues who claim they are your friends but instead are back stabbers and big-time liars, think from their point of view. Are they trying to maximize their benefits, because it's normal as that is how they have evolved? We cannot blame them much. Are they looking for some benefit out of the relationship because most relationships in workplaces (and in this world) are transactional in nature? Or are you expecting too much in a relationship?

If you understand the above-mentioned points fully and apply in your day-to-day work life, you will establish a rationale to overcome the situation without letting the relationship with colleagues getting affected much. Even then, if things are slipping much out of hand, you need to ask yourself, 'will you be happy if you elude this situation?' If yes, leave it at that. Do not force yourself to fix the situation if it is going too much out of control. Even if you work for your dream company, it is okay to let go of it if things are taking toll on your mental or emotional health. And if you are already in the phase of loneliness, do act on the steps suggested above to tackle it. Loneliness does not only lead to various physical and mental illnesses and poor work outcomes; it breaks you from inside and makes you weak. It hampers your resilience to manage difficulties and hampers your positive temperament to live and enjoy life. Hence, act on it seriously and make sure you do not let it influence you (negatively) too much.

ASSESS YOUR LONELINESS AT WORK

There are two ways in which our loneliness can be discovered—either through a counselling session where a mental health professional talks to you to understand what you are really going through or through a self-reported test. One of the most popular assessments on loneliness is the UCLA Loneliness Scale, which helps you figure out if you feel lonely. Fill it up to find out your loneliness levels (Refer to the appendix given at the end of this chapter).

Q: How can I offer emotional first aid to lonely peers?

A: First of all, stay away from making armchair diagnosis. You might or might not have gone through the experience of loneliness. If you have ever felt lonely, acute or chronic, your experiences might be different from others. Hence, irrespective of whether you have ever been through loneliness or not, listen to their narratives of loneliness. If you simply ask 'Are you fine?' they will end up saying 'Yes, I am fine.' They might never come upfront and tell you, fearing the anticipated reaction from you. Instead ask them what they feel, right now and on day-to-day basis. Listen to them when they speak. Let them speak as much as possible. They want somebody to listen to them without judging them. Do not say things like 'It is normal to feel this way' or 'I am sure you will be fine' or worse suggestion, 'Be strong.' Instead tell them, 'I know it is hard on you', 'I have been through it once and it was so difficult', 'Though I cannot share your pain, I can talk to you and maybe we can work on a solution.' Tell them that you understand this is tricky and difficult situation for them. Reach out to them multiple times, but not to an extent that your nudges might become annoying for them. So, tackle it accordingly. At times, people around you do not even tell you if something is wrong with them, even if it's your close family members or a friend, forget colleagues. Hence, it is important for us to observe any noticeable change in their behaviour and act on it. Reach out to them. Do not delay because you have got no time. Convince them to seek help of a psychologist or a psychiatrist.

Q: Is loneliness a disease?

A: 'No'. Loneliness is an *emotion*, a negative, undesirable and an unpleasant one. It occurs when we are unhappy with our current social connections and we crave for more meaningful relationships in life, or when there is an absence of such relationships altogether. Having said that, if loneliness lingers over a period of time, it definitely leads to various short- and long-term illnesses.

Q: Are introverts more prone to loneliness?

A: No, there is no correlation between personality and loneliness. Loneliness can happen to an extrovert and an introvert indiscriminately. Though an old school of thought has established that people who are shy or not sociable tend to feel more loneliness, there have been many research who have decried this idea empirically.

Q: Is loneliness similar to isolation, solitude and aloneness?

A: Often, we confuse loneliness with terms such as solitude, isolation, aloneness, etc.

Loneliness is more dangerous as compared to isolation. Loneliness happens when you might have umpteen people around you to meet or talk to, but the quality of interaction is missing. Loneliness is quite an intriguing phenomenon. In a room of 1,000 people, you may feel lonely. Hence, it's about the quality of social interaction and not the quantity. Therefore, loneliness is referred to as subjective isolation (objective isolation indicates the frequency of your social contact).

Isolation happens when you meet people less frequently; for example, you are in a job wherein you do not have much scope of interaction, say a travelling job. Similarly, solitude and loneliness are two different things altogether. While solitude is a positive emotion and is by choice, loneliness is a negative emotion and does not occur by choice. Solitude is a pleasant emotion, and when in solitude, humans do not crave meaningful social interactions, like when in loneliness. Solitude or aloneness is, in fact, an important feeling to experience. In fact, many schools of thoughts[10] encourage learning aloneness.

---

[10] https://thehill.com/changing-america/well-being/mental-health/484368-the-case-for-being-alone https://www.forbes.com/sites/amymorin/2017/08/05/7-science-backed-reasons-you-should-spend-more-time-alone/?sh=4be19e661b7e

Aloneness or solitude involves enjoying one's own company and not getting bored being alone. Aloneness is said to be addictive for the fact that it encourages and leads us to the positive path of spirituality, to know oneself better, be able to calm down and relax and reflect on life's philosophy. While these might be related to each other in some way or the other, they are not precisely loneliness.

APPENDIX

UCLA LONELINESS SCALE ADAPTED FROM © DR DANIEL RUSSELL[11]

Instructions

The following statements describe how people sometimes feel. For each statement, please indicate how often you think the way expressed using the numbers below. There are no right or wrong answers.

---

[11] https://www.aarp.org/personal-growth/transitions/info-09-2010/How-Lonely-are-You.html

At Work	Never	Rarely	Sometimes	Always
1. How often do you feel unhappy doing so many things alone?	①	②	③	④
2. How often do you feel you have no one to talk to?	①	②	③	④
3. How often do you feel you cannot tolerate being so alone?	①	②	③	④
4. How often do you feel as if no one understands you?	①	②	③	④
5. How often do you find yourself waiting for people to call or write?	①	②	③	④
6. How often do you feel completely alone?	①	②	③	④
7. How often do you feel unable to reach out and communicate with those around you?	①	②	③	④
8. How often do you feel starved for company?	①	②	③	④
9. How often do you feel it is difficult for you to make friends?	①	②	③	④
10. How often do you feel shut out and excluded by others?	①	②	③	④

Source: UCLA Loneliness Scale Version

Scoring

Check your scores to figure out what you are currently going through. Your total score is computed by adding up the scores of each question. The 'average loneliness' score on the measure is 25. A score higher than 25 reflects high level of loneliness.

As mentioned earlier, an average level of loneliness is still acceptable. Given the current lifestyle, it will not be an exaggeration to say that we all are lonely to some extent. However, if you fall in the category of high to very high levels of loneliness, it is time to reflect on things and take action. The latter part of the chapter concerns with dealing with a high level of loneliness. If your scores indicate a very high level of loneliness, that is, 30 or above, you need to meet a mental health expert without any ado. Do not panic, but do not ignore, at the same time, assuming it will recuperate on its own.

✳ 4 ✳

COPING WITH STRESS

'Stress', the word has become a part of our day-to-day vocabulary nowadays. A true physicist would say that stress is the force acting on the unit area of a material object and *Britannica*[1] goes a step further to define it as '... force per unit area within materials that arises from externally applied forces ...'. The same definition applies in the world of psychology and human behaviour as well, where stress is developed as a result of external forces and/or changes in the circumstances. The transition from college to work definitely counts as a drastic change in circumstance and we witness rising levels of stress in people in such a situation.

Once, in an organizational behaviour class, I asked my students, 'What is that one thing that makes you similar to others sitting in the class?' Their answer, 'The fact that we all are stressed out and depressed,' cracked me up. While it really sounded funny, in reality, it isn't. Frankly, stress is one of the heavily discussed topics. Stress is inevitable and there is no escape. All of us are exposed to stressors every day. However, some situations stress us out more than the others. While I am writing this book sitting inside my office cabin, there is a pandemic going on outside that

---

[1] https://www.britannica.com/science/stress-physics

has affected and smashed the entire world. The pandemic period has been nothing but full of stress and anxiety. Scholars and practitioners have taken this opportunity to investigate more about the impact of stress on people, both at work and in personal space. One of the observations in this regard that definitely stood out to me was the results of the Market Watch Research Survey done among the US workers. Nearly 70 per cent of the US workers said that COVID–19 is the 'most stressful time' of their entire professional careers, even when compared to events such as the Great Recession and the 11 September terrorist attacks. Surprised? I am sure you're not. All of us have been sailing in the same boat, after all.

STRESS AT WORK

For one of my research projects, I particularly wanted to dig a little deeper and understand if managing stress is really a pervasive issue for young working professionals. I asked around 450 working professionals 'What bothers you most at work?' After analysing the responses, there were five major trends observed as a result of word cloud analysis.

The dissolution of work–life boundaries and its consequent strain was one of the major observations that came out consistently.

The next couple of trends that stood out were the building up of frustration and physical and psychological exhaustion.

The overall feeling of gloominess and loneliness were the last two that completed the top five trends. Frankly, these trends do not baffle me.

They all have been in the heavily discussed topics in psychology. However, if you notice, the common denominator for all the above-mentioned issues is *stress*. Work may become stressful for us if we perceive too many challenges, demands and threats in the environment that we are not able to deal.

STRESS AND 'FIGHT' VERSUS 'FLIGHT'

Imagine a casual day when your boss asked you to make an impromptu presentation in front of the board members. Or you heard bad news from the client you were not prepared for. Do you feel sudden rush in your body in such unexpected situations? Your breathing becomes heavier, face becomes pale and/or you feel sudden weakness in gut or legs. Do you suddenly become more attentive and your eyes get dilated? All of us do. This is a natural response of our body when we see a life-threatening situation. This is our bodily response of fight or flight, also known as acute stress response. Either we fight, in other words, approach the situation, or we flee, that is, avoid the situation. Both are different from each other and are separate constructs.

Fight or flight can be considered as a bodily coping mechanism with threats, a response to something that is terrifying, either mentally or physically. There is an evolutionary explanation behind this phenomenon. Our ancestors used to be surrounded by various sorts of threats including attack from huge animals. It was matter of life or death. As their entire life was surrounded by dangerous species, to survive better, they developed the fight or flight coping mechanism. This instinct is very much intact in us even now. Through this mechanism, once our brain senses a life-threatening situation, it prepares to cope with it. 'Stress', in this regard, acts as a signal to the brain, which then releases a stress hormone, whose objective is to create an alarm in us. Thanks to our ancestors, we have a mechanism to prepare ourselves physically and biologically when encountered with stressors. Either it prepared their body to stay and deal with a threat (i.e., fight) or to run away to safety (i.e., flight).

The way stress was defined traditionally is in stark contrast with its modern definition. The old definitions explicitly indicated the positive connotation that was attached with stress at that point. It is intriguing to know that stress was a biological phenomenon against a physical or mental threat that was created to work in our favour (to alarm us of dangers), instead of working against us. The modern definition of stress, however, speaks volumes about the current interpretation of the phenomenon. The contemporary scholars define it as 'a feeling of emotional strain and pressure'. Shocking, isn't it? Modern lives have distorted our understanding of events and processes that once were considered as a gift to humankind. In fact, the definition of 'life-threatening situations' has changed totally. Nowadays, disagreement with peers, argument with the boss, fear of missing out, fear of rejection, exclusion or unknown stresses us out, including many other things. In fact, we have created a gamut of 'modern' issues that stress us out.

The following two things are mainly important in this regard.

1. **Accept that stress is positive:** Many years ago, we started off on a note that stress is positive and helpful for our survival. However, as kids growing

up, we never heard people telling us that stress is positive. We commonly hear people saying, 'Stress is extremely bad for our emotional, mental and physical health,' 'Stress can be severely detrimental to life,' and 'Don't stress yourself over things'. No doubt stress has become one of the most common reasons for psychosomatic illnesses in the current times. High stress levels lead to cardiovascular diseases, lifestyle disorders (such as hypothyroidism), sexual illnesses, strokes and what not. If stress was supposed to be helpful to our survival, why did it become detrimental to our lives?

Note that over the years, our body has evolved to respond in a certain way (fight or flight) every time it encounters danger. Whether it is an attack from an animal or nomophobia, what we define as 'dangerous' or 'stressful' for ourselves is completely upon us. Our body will react accordingly. It is saddening that, in current times, not getting the 'best employee of the year' award is comparable to hunting for food and saving ourselves from man-eaters. So, who is to be blamed? It goes without saying, we have not quite understood the importance of acute stress in our lives. Unfortunately, we have not fully accepted that those heated arguments with clients/boss/colleagues or that two hours extra work that we did the other day for free are part and parcel of life. These events, by no means, are and should become a source of stress for us. These events should not control our lives. We really have not quite understood it.

So, first things first, 'don't stress yourself over stress!' Not all kinds of stress are bad. Not all the things that go wrong or did not go as per your plan are bad for you. Stop thinking that stress is bad. The important thing to remember is the fact that we, human beings, are biologically configured to adapt to stress. Hence, know that our bodies are designed in a way to handle stress. To help you truly grasp the extent of risks that perceptions of stress threatens us with, I would like to allude you to a research[2] conducted on 28,753 US adults, where amount of stress, its perceived impacts on health and death rate of individuals were recorded. It was found that people who had recorded perceived health impacts had an increased risk of premature death. In simple words, people who felt stress is bad for them died prematurely.

Take the notion that 'stress sucks my life' out of your head. By no means it is going to hamper your life unless you do not tackle acute stress properly and let it become chronic in nature. Yes, just like in the world of physics where stress over a continued period of time can cause morphological changes, continuous exposure to stress especially when it is not being handled carefully or being bottled up can result in chronic stress. In a workplace setting, prolonged exposure to stress results in job burnout (highly common among fresh recruits), which can have severe impacts on the emotional, mental and physical well-being of a person.

- The person might feel emotionally exhausted, that is, the feeling of being emotionally drained or used up at the end of the day. It may further get accompanied by morning fatigue, loss of patience, frustration build up or simply feeling that you are working too hard on your job.

- One might also feel detached or depersonalized from their colleagues which might surface up as

---

[2] https://www.ncbi.nlm.nih.gov/pmc/articles/PMC3374921/

insensitiveness towards peers, carelessness bordering on indifference to the professional surrounding.

- Both the above symptoms may lead to reduced sense of accomplishment—a decreased sense of competence and successful achievement in work.

Now that you have comprehensively read (and understood, hopefully) the idea of stress, it will be easier for you to leverage the benefits of fight or flight.

2. **Train your brain**: Yes, fight or flight are great indicators to understand the source of stress and our reactions to them. Moreover, it gives cues to our body to prepare for an action or coping mechanism to a surrounding threat. Once understood fully, it can help you lead a happy and healthy life. However, there are two important points to note here. First, not all fight or flight reactions are good and helpful. As discussed previously, this acute response to each and every stressor is not good. If you get stressed every time you meet that colleague you hate, know that you have trained yourself to get bothered by things that are not significant. It simply indicates you have conditioned your brain to react negatively to a situation (in this situation, that colleague) that is not worth your time. Recall, how fight or flight response was meant for 'life-threatening situation'. It is up to you, how you differentiate between a dangerous and a non-dangerous situation. Not being able to make an extra impression on your boss should not invoke stress hormones in your body. You got me, right! Define your priorities. Draw boundary between significant and non-significant events, things,

humans, places or objects. This will help you keep a check on identifying what is really 'life-threatening' for you. Hence, choose wisely and react accordingly. Not every incident is worth your reaction.

Second, start observing your own behaviour on a day-to-day basis. Make mental and/or written notes in a diary about work stressors that stress you out a lot and how you react to it. Once you have collected enough data, you will get a fair idea on some convergent points, that is, most commonly occurring situation that your brain feels is dangerous. It could be as small as not getting your favourite breakfast at office canteen or as big as being in the middle of a firing process. Fight or flight reactions help us keep a check on our own behaviour and, hence, allows us the chance to improve or control pre-emptively. Once you have filled enough pages of your diary, you are now clearly in a position to decide if it is worth losing your temper, letting that stress hormone run through your body up and down or letting it affect your physical or emotional well-being. Once you have identified events that bother you the most, revisit the first point, that is, deciding if the events are worth a fight or flight reaction. If not, then start conditioning yourself. *Explain to* yourself, for example, 'it is okay to not being able to meet the target.' *Convince* yourself, for example, 'I am reacting in this manner as I have trained myself to be scared of this situation.' *Remind* yourself, for example, 'In the past, every time I goofed up, I was shouted at. That is the reason I react in a certain manner. However, this is a very regular situation and really not life-threatening.' And last but not least, *affirm* yourself that you are capable of improving yourself. Repeat this exercise. You will definitely witness a positive change in your behaviour. An example of the diary page includes:

	Explain	Convince	Remind	Affirm
Event 1	Disagreement in office WhatsApp groups	It is normal to have disagreements in social groups, especially work groups, as opinions are subjective and are affected by cognitive experiences. Everybody/my teammates can choose to agree to disagree. Disagreements fuel new thoughts and new knowledge.	I am feeling jittery about it as I have trained my mind to react negatively to disagreements.	This must have started during my college days. I was always told to be right and was expected to know everything. This definitely is not a lethal/critical situation to lose my mind on.	I will learn to listen to and accept my teammates' ideas.
Event 2				
Event 3				
Event 4				
Event 5				

Source: The author.

ACTIVITY: THINKING OF EVENTS THAT OFTEN STRESS YOU OUT THE MOST

Note that stress hampers your productivity in personal and professional life, whether the reason is personal or professional. A new job, especially when joined as a rookie, may bring myriad of changes which inevitably will lead to stress. Now you know our body triggers the release of hormones that prepare us either to stay and deal with the threat or to run away to safety during a stressful situation, that is, *fight or flight.*

APPROACH OR AVOID?

Though there are several ways in which you may attempt to cope with a stressor at work (successfully or unsuccessfully), two main coping mechanisms include approach and avoidance method. These two coping mechanisms are mutually exclusive, and which one you choose depends upon several things, such as the situation you are in and your personality. However, there are no strong correlations between personality and specific coping mechanisms; that is, if you an introvert, you will not necessarily always choose a particular mechanism to cope with the stressor. Hence, it depends a lot more on the situation than anything else. 'Approach coping is any behavioral, cognitive, or emotional activity that is directed toward a threat (e.g., problem-solving or seeking information). Avoidance is any behavioral, cognitive, or emotional activity directed away from a threat (e.g., denial, withdrawal).'[3] For example, if

---

[3] https://www.sciencedirect.com/topics/medicine-and-dentistry/coping-strategies

you do not like this colleague of yours, and every time you bump into them in the corridor, you get upset. You may either approach this situation or avoid it since it stresses you out. Under approach coping mechanism, you would tend to reappraise the situation.

For example, you rethink about this colleague positively or put yourself in this colleague's shoes to try and empathize better. You may also think of talking it out. Under the avoidance mechanism, you would distance yourself from this colleague and change your route every time you see him/her. Needless to say, researchers have established approach coping mechanism as a better mechanism of coping. The argument here is that avoidance coping mechanism is not practical in every situation, as we cannot keep running away from the problems all the time. At work, one has to carry a solution-oriented approach and face the issue head-on instead of avoiding it. However, I suggest one should be flexible enough to deal with stressors in either way (approach or avoid), depending upon the circumstances and demands. I want to emphasize the fact that stressors come in all shapes and sizes. Not all stressors have a significant impact on our lives. Why not prioritize the situation and approach issues that need a solution and avoid the ones that are silly and insignificant? However, you need to be smart enough to judge whether the situation requires you to approach the problem or avoid it. Having said that, prepare yourself with both types of mechanisms. While I do not endorse that avoidance coping is maladaptive (established by many researches), I wouldn't suggest you to depend on it entirely. Learn to face difficult or upsetting situations, confront issues, face your fears head-on, and work on resolving them instead of avoiding them. And when the situation seems to be unworthy of your time and energy, you may choose to avoid it.

To deal with stressors, there are two positive and life-changing coping mechanisms that you should know—emotions-focused coping and problem-focused coping. 'Emotion-focused coping' is aimed at minimizing distress triggered by stressors. Because there are many ways to reduce distress, emotion-focused coping includes a wide range of responses, ranging from self-soothing (e.g., relaxation, seeking emotional support), to expression of negative emotion (e.g., yelling, crying), to a focus on negative thoughts (e.g., rumination), to attempts to escape stressful situations (e.g., avoidance, denial, wishful thinking).

> Problem-focused coping is directed at the stressor itself: taking steps to remove or to evade it, or to diminish its impact if it cannot be evaded. For example, if layoffs are expected, an employee's problem-focused coping might include saving money, applying for other jobs, obtaining training to enhance hiring prospects, or working harder at the current job to reduce the likelihood of being let go.[4]

Next time you are in a stressful situation that significantly impacts you and is worth solving, try emotional- or problem-focused coping. Reappraise the situation or the problem differently (say from a more positive lens) to reduce its impact on yourself, that is, emotional coping, or confront or deal

[4] https://www.annualreviews.org/doi/pdf/10.1146/annurev.psych.093008.100352

with the stressor directly and work to eliminate it, that is, problem coping.

Now that you know about emotional- and problem-focused coping, you should know when to follow what at work. First things first, evaluate the situation or the stressor. What does it look like? Controllable or uncontrollable. Once you get this understanding, it will be easy for you to take the right action. If the situation seems uncontrollable (or unchangeable), it is better you follow emotions-focused strategies, and for controllable (or changeable) situations, follow problem-focused strategies.

RESILIENCE

Have you ever played with those round-bottomed dolls called the wobbly man which, no matter how many times you hit, would always bounce back and never fall down? Yes, it will swing more and more as you strike it stronger, but still, finally come back to rest, upright in its original position after swinging for a while. Ironically, the wobbly man, in complete disregard to its name, is the epitome example of resilience. So, what is resilience? Resilience refers to how well you can deal with and bounce back from the stressful events. It is an effective coping mechanism with stressors, and returning to equilibrium, or 'homeostasis', quickly after stress offset.[5]

---

[5] https://www.brainfacts.org/Diseases-and-Disorders/Mental-Health/ 2018/What-is-stress-resilience-and-can-it-be-learned-071018#:~:text =I%20prefer%20to%20conceptualize%20%E2%80%9Cstress,optim ization%E2%80%9D%20rather%20than%20stress%20resilience.

Have you ever wondered why some of your colleagues, equally affected as you with an event, say, with a failed business deal, bounce back much faster than you do and are far less affected than you? The explanation is that they may be having better resilience skills than you. To be able to learn how to deal with stressors is one of the initial steps to lead a happy and healthy life. Having resilience does not mean you will not get stressed about events. It simply means you will be easily able to come out of it without letting yourself get affected too much. The important point to note is different individuals have different levels of resilience in them. The higher the endurance or resilience towards stress, the better will be your adapting capabilities in the face of adversities.

THE GOOD NEWS!

Unlike personality traits, resilience is a continuous process, where circumstances and changes help you to adapt, learn and improve. Early career brings you a lot of tough and stressful situations.

Therefore, as a young manager, it is apt to ask oneself, 'How resilient am I?'

Do you take actions to solve a problem at work, to fix things that are causing the problems, or do you simply give up? Can you calm yourself down when you are feeling over-whelmed or just let yourself run into a state of anxiety? Do you charge at a problem head on like an angry blinded-by-red bull, or do you take the time to look at your options and alternative solutions? Do you have faith in yourself and the universe, reframing the situation as a challenge to learn

MASTERING BEHAVIOUR

and bounce back to an improved state of yourself? Do you retrospect on how to handle it better next time, be it a jab with the client or an unsuccessful deal?

These questions are in no way easy to answer at one go, as they are all respective. You need to delve deeper into yourself and get a true understanding of how you behave under stressful conditions of a crisis. If most of the answers in the above questions are affirmative, then you are already on the path of resilience and you need to keep on trudging on it taking learning all the way consistently. If most of the answers are negative, you are in a rough spot, and it is time to buckle up and have a close watch on yourself.

In the context of a team in a professional setting, it becomes even more important to be cognizant of not only the resilience of yourself but also the resilience of the team as a whole, which basically depends on the resilience of its team members. Negative emotions, harboured by a non-resilient member, can easily be contagious and if not managed with care, may impact the entire team.

So, what can be done to build resilience? Some consistent practices and careful efforts, such as the following, can go a long way to build and improve resilience.

SELF-AWARENESS IS THE KEY

Being aware of your inner self is the most basic step to bring in changes in oneself. Though it is important to know more about yourself, it is not as straightforward as it sounds. It is a bit complicated, as people perceive themselves as what they want to become instead of who they are. How many of us surely know our weakness or flaws? Even if we are aware of the flaws, have we accepted them as part of our behaviour that might be bothering others, not just us? To modify your behaviour and work upon improvement areas, first know your limitations. Common sense, isn't it? Unless you know you are weak in presentation skills, how will you allocate more time in improving your present-ation skills? Or unless you know you are a good debater, you would not be confident to participate in a boardroom debate.

Hence, start with the most basic. Know what affects you the most at work. Make notes of peers or events that instigate or trigger you. Know your strength and weakness. Unless you are not sure about what affects you the most, you would not be able to mitigate its cause.

RECOGNIZE AND ACCEPT YOUR EMOTIONAL STATE

We were taught to focus on good things and avoid bad ones. I am telling you the exact opposite. Ask yourself—what are you feeling right now? Positive or negative, accept it instead of avoiding or suppressing it. The idea here is to be aware of yourself and your emotional state. To accept what you are feeling (whether positive or negative), first learn to recognize and identify your emotions. If today is not a good day for you, ask yourself, 'Am I feeling blue today?' If yes, just deal with it as usual. It is natural to be surrounded by positive and negative emotions from time to time. It is absolutely normal to feel gloomy, sad, envious, etc. These are the universal emotions. Everybody goes through it; you are no different. The trick here is to stay and deal with the change instead of resisting it, leading to a better endurance in difficult times.

DO NOT BE IN HASTE TO LABEL

Very often, we tend to pigeonhole our situations as 'good' or 'bad'. I suggest avoiding putting a label on your situation. A judgement of good or bad will not help you; it will only make you more anxious. Treat it as an ordinary feeling. You never know what seems wrong or bad at this point is meant to create something excellent for the future. I am sure it has happened with all of us, a lot of times. What felt like a 'serious concern' to me brought me new stress. Whenever you feel 'why me?' wait for the right time to get your answers. Patience is the key here. Whether it is a good thing or a bad thing, whether it is a threat or an opportunity, who knows?! The only truth that you know is that you are feeling it. Hence, stop being concerned about your situation without knowing it thoroughly. Stop getting all worked up with events without knowing the consequences fully.

DO NOT COPY OTHERS' COPING MECHANISMS

It is essential to accept that different people have different coping mechanisms; that is, some might fight while some might flee when encountered with a stressor. Hence, it would be unfair to make a comparison of your coping mechanism to your cohorts'. Reaction to the same stimulus can be very different for different people. What feels right for someone might not sit well with you. Note that not every coping strategy is meant for you. If you do not explore the 'right' coping strategies for yourself and just follow others' paths, you might end up getting disappointed. So, it is vital to find out what works for you. For example, many students have told me that sleeping helps them escape the issue for a while and helps them in reappraising the situation with positivity once they wake up. Know that while it might work for some, it is not a universal situation. Some of us do get more anxious after waking up without issues at hand being resolved, let alone the issue being reappraised. Hence, do not copy them. Figure out your coping mechanism from stressors rather than aping others.

AVOID AVOIDANCE-COPING AS FAR AS POSSIBLE

Do you know these people around you who think that a cup of coffee will solve all their problems? At workplaces, not just caffeine, but relying too much on smoking to 'deal' with issues is quite common again. Resorting to high dosages of caffeine or nicotine is just going to delay the stressors, not help you overcome them. Some other commonly seen avoidance strategies include altogether avoiding people causing stress, burying heads in the sand like the ostrich in danger, entirely depending on others to solve their problems. These are not very effective strategies if you want to build endurance. Some more examples of avoidance coping include avoiding the person you hate the most at college, switch careers as you hate your manager or blaming others for situations you failed to resolve. As mentioned earlier, depend on avoidance coping when you feel the situation is not significant enough and will not impact you in the short or long term in any way.

COMMUNICATE

Take full advantage of your network. Think of your support bases, talk to your confidants, vent it out with your figure of attachment, reach out and relate to your support system; essentially, speak to people who listen to you and understand you without judging you. If you have figured out that 'attachment figure' for yourself who gives you enough space to speak, you are sorted. Building a trustworthy social circle in this regard is crucial. That does not mean you need 10 people around you all the time. Just that one person who is good at confronting emotional expressions and is patient enough to listen to you, you are good to go. A good friend will take time out from his/her schedule just for you, support you and stand beside you through your thick and thin.

PAUSE AND BREATHE

It is important to slow down, pause and take a deep breath. Be in the moment; really be aware of your surroundings, focus yourself on the single task of breathing and wipe your restless mind clean of thoughts for a change. After you wake up, a daily morning mindfulness session will help your mind focus on positive energy and boost your morale to deal with any stressors throughout the day. Understand what the child in you needs and make it come to life. Take out the time to disconnect from the world, from your devices post work hours and connect to nature. Talk to your plants or pets if you have any. Do not rush always; take small steps. The crux is to do tasks that are meaningful to you. Whether you have enrolled yourself in an MBA programme or joined your dream company, take it easy. You are not expected to be productive all the time. Cut some slack there. Take a moment for yourself if you are in a professional setting. Follow these, especially when you are too stressed out about something.

All my life, I heard people suggesting that I become a multitasker. Trust me, being a multitasker is overrated. If it does not suit your requirements and makes you lose your calm, be it work or otherwise, be a mono-tasker. Do one thing at a time; do it bit by bit. Do not get overwhelmed and overburdened in order to prove your capabilities as a multitasker. Monotasking helps us remain calm, free from stress and helps in building focus and concentration.

PHYSICAL AROUSAL/EXERCISE

Physical activities that pump or psych you up is a daily necessity, even if it is done for 15 minutes. A simple stroll in a nearby park or a few Surya Namaskars will go a long way to release some of the tensions and make you more light and agile, all geared up to face and endure your stressor.

PRAY OR MEDITATE

Follow the path of spirituality and give yourself time to retrospect and focus. It helps a lot in calming your inner turmoil. In this scenario, few chants per day or simply a self-reflective session through mediation may guide you to the path of spirituality. Be it a chant, calming music, mediation or 10 deep breaths with closed eyes, anything that helps you connect with your inner self shall suffice the purpose. You basically need some 'me time'. Figure out the me-time window, even if it is 10 minutes a day. During this time, you should detach yourself from things around you.

BE GRATEFUL FOR THINGS AROUND YOU

This is not the first time you must be reading about the bene-fits of the following gratefulness. Practising gratefulness is another way in which you can cultivate resilience skills. Look at every crisis, every stressor as an opportunity to redeem yourself, improve yourself, challenge yourself and build a better version of yourself. Gold, after all, is purified when passed through the fire. Simple acts of gratefulness can help you a long way. Every night, before you sleep, think of good things that happened to you that day. Tell yourself the reason to be happy. Try to make people feel good about themselves. Extend support to people who are vulnerable or needy, if possible. Care for animals around you. Thank the universe for letting you eat good meals. Contribute in whichever way you can.

When you are new to the workplace, every decision is spiked with uncertainty, every activity laced with stressors. No wonder resilience has landed right on top of the list of must-have skills now. Not just for executives, it is a necessary skillset for everyone, for each one of us and for all of us. Do not practice all the suggestions mentioned above simultaneously. Too much of newness in daily routine can be overwhelming. Try a few things at a time. Once you feel you are becoming better in that specific aspect, move on to the next few. Working on building resilience is undoubtedly not a cakewalk. However, constant practice and incorporating these suggestions sincerely will help you go a long way.

Despite putting efforts, if you feel you are failing to navigate the difficulties, remember that you are not alone in this journey!

Q&A

Q: If I wanted to know my colleagues' ethical standards or, in other words, to what extent he/she willing to compromise his/her principles, I would put that colleague in a high-stake situation which would also be stressful. Because, I think, in a peaceful environment, they can easily pretend. After all, it is in a crisis we know both our strengths and weaknesses because we are pushed to our extremes and have no choice. I would like to know if my conclusions are wrong and why. This was how I have been evaluating people for years, and I thought this was a right matrix.

A: People tend to behave differently from what they actually are under stressful conditions. Observe them and collect information about them. In case of consistent behaviour across situations, it can be concluded as internal. If the behaviour is distinct in distinct situations, it can possibly be due to external factors. Based on your observation, you may conclude if a particular behaviour is due to disposition or situation. Note that this inference should not be drawn based on one or two incidents. Handful of information leads to biased conclusions. Remember, we are supposed to assess them, not judge them.

Q: In my workplace, I get anxious only in certain situations and due to certain people only. One of the issues that I found out was that being lied to by teammates in certain situations acts as a trigger for me, and then I lose every sort of control I have on my emotions. But this does not happen every time, because over the years, I have learnt to have a control on my reactions to situations. If only select individuals or a particular situation causes my anxiety, is it not due to external issues instead of being an internal issue, that is, my attitude or personality?

Also, just like there are situations where I feel too much, there have been situations where I do not feel at all. I also have those kinds of mood swings where I am all jolly and the next moment the gloomiest person in the room. Does all of this make me a bipolar person? If so, I believe it is not a good thing, and can it be changed?

A: If the issue recurs with the same trigger, irrespective of who it is (peer who is close to you or acquaintance), it can be because of your personality (your internal issue). As you rightly pointed out, over the years, it seems you have learned to curb your emotions. Though you have learned to suppress it, it might trigger a lot of times when the situation is not too favourable.

I believe it has more to do with your high emotional instability. Start making an immediate note of it every time it happens. You should first know what the actual stressor/cause of your mood swing is.

Do it at least for a month, and then connect the dots to see if you can interpret the source of the problem. If you are not able to figure out one or two common sources, highly likely it is due to your trait. Though it cannot be changed fully, you can learn to control it. Do not worry about it being good or bad as long as it is not affecting you or others much.

* 5 *

EXPLORING RELATIONSHIP POSSIBILITIES IN WORK EXCHANGES

A young colleague of mine, a fresh graduate from a top-notch college, recently joined my organization. She told me, 'People here work for incentives. They push their boundaries only when external rewards are given. That is not how I work. I work for my inner satisfaction. I do not really need rewards attached to the projects I volunteer for. How can I collaborate with such people who are not like me?'

While I am not baffled by my young colleague's attitude at work (everyone has preferences), I am certainly concerned about situations when such strong choices may backfire on her. But again, I must not judge her. During my initial experience, being a young employee, I withdrew myself from multiple projects as I was not comfortable with my team members' working style. To give you an example, I was quite involved in a research project for which I had volunteered along with three more colleagues. We all were assigned targets and deadlines. Being strict on deadlines, I religiously followed up with them. In fact, missing deadlines puts me in a state of anxiety. To avoid that, I ensure

my work is always completed on time; in fact, ahead of the deadline, if possible. On the day after the deadline, I emailed everybody following up on their progress and to decide on the next steps. To my surprise, nobody responded for the next five days. That came as a shock to me as I consider responding to emails on time an important indicator of one's integrity towards the profession. Failing to receive responses, I pinged them on WhatsApp to know about the status of their work. Another surprise shook me. Nobody had even completed 50 per cent of the assigned tasks. I was appalled to see my colleagues taking it so casually. This kept recurring for around three to four months, post which I finally gave up. I was honest with them about my working style, and I told them I could not work on this project anymore as my working style does not match theirs. While they were not entirely happy with what I said, they were kind enough to accept it as a valid reason for me to leave the project.

Two things to note here. First, at work, especially as a rookie, you do not have much control over situations. You do not have the choice to pick and choose your team members. You cannot decide whom you want to work with. Whether you like it or not, you are expected to suck it up and work with people irrespective of your working style's incoherence. Second, everybody is different in some way, good or bad. And everybody has idiosyncrasies. So, if you feel you will find a perfect teammate, it will never happen. Yes, you may find one or two people whose frequency perfectly matches with yours. But your working styles and preferences do not sync with your *entire* team.

IT IS AN EXCHANGE RELATIONSHIP

In a classical social-psychological theory, commonly known as 'social exchange theory', the exchange between two parties was emphasized. This theory studies social behaviour in the interaction of two parties that implement a cost-benefit analysis to determine risks and benefits, especially at workplaces. Work-related social exchange involves economic relationships that occurs when each party has goods that the other parties value. Social exchange theory suggests that these cost–benefit calculations occur in professional associations and in romantic relationships, friendships and ephemeral relationships as simple as exchanging words with a customer at the cash register.

Social exchange theory suggests that if the relationship costs are higher than the rewards, such as if a lot of effort or time was put into a relationship and not reciprocated, the relationship may be terminated or abandoned. So, note that while you have certain expectations in terms of outputs in your relationship with your colleagues (e.g., timely response, adhering to deadlines, intrinsically motivated to perform tasks), your colleagues expect something out of the exchange too.

Be it working style, value congruence or expectations match, everybody at work is seeking something in exchange. After all, the relationships are mostly transactional at work. Now, imagine a situation where neither you are satisfied and happy with others, nor are they with you. But both of you are expected to work together by hook or crook. Imagine the level of animosity you two must have created for each other. But then, can you tell your boss, 'I do not want to work with this guy as I do not really like the way he

116

works?' Probably yes, if you were a veteran. Unfortunately, you are a newcomer, and the bargaining power is not in your hand.

SO, IS THERE ANY SOLUTION?

Can it be possible that you *change* the way you look at the person (reappraise) by exploring the possibilities of positive interactions or, at least, change the opportunity to maximize your gains in the relationship instead of hating on that co-worker?

It is not easy initially. As a first-time manager, you see things from your lens. You expect everybody to be proper, everybody to meet your expectation. You get disappointed quickly. You get hurt easily. You have no experience dealing with people who are different from you. Simple, because so far you got to choose whom you liked! During college, you never went out with people who were entirely different from you. You hung out with people who had some commonalities. Isn't it? Now, there is a sudden shift in the environment. People look different. They look unfamiliar. They are not your friends. They recognize you for the temperament you carry at work (and ignore you if you come across as unaccommodating!) As you grow old in the organization, people start knowing you for your hard work, skills, abilities and competencies. But that takes time to build, even if you hail from a top-notch institute. For your colleagues, all the newcomers seem alike. There are no explicit differentiating qualities. And it is justified as they only have less information about you.

So, it is totally up to you what you want to come across as. Why not build a more positive image and create a long-lasting impression on people by being nice to them, accommodating and accepting them for what they are? One such way to learn this technique is through the popular MBTI personality type framework.[1] To change your perspectives, you first need to understand the 'types' MBTI offers. Second, through these types of people at workplace, you decide who is who and how they can be dealt with. Note that we are not pigeonholing people here. We are just trying to understand their working styles better, and for this, there is no better framework than MBTI. Third, we will reflect on each type's critical areas and learn about the potential positive and negative encounters with each category (and prepare ourselves accordingly at work). Fourth, we will learn some tips and tricks to explore the possibilities of positive communication and interaction with people who we 'perceive' as different from us.

KNOW THY COLLEAGUES: MBTI®

MBTI[2] is a great tool to understand people and their personality types. It breaks down people's personality type into four different dichotomies for an easier understanding of their working style. In fact, it is one of the most popularly taken tests across the globe and quite frequently used in workplaces.

In this segment, we will understand the MBTI framework in the context of organizations. The idea is simple. As a first-time manager, how do you understand and interpret your type and that of your colleagues? This framework will give

---

[1] https://mbtitraininginstitute.myersbriggs.org/
[2] Note that MBTI is the original work of myersbriggs.org.

MASTERING BEHAVIOUR

you a better idea for understanding why your colleagues seem to be different from you in terms of their working style, decision-making, handling conversations and their overall behaviour. Moreover, MBTI can help you understand how to deal with their differences. The following segments will also offer you tips and tricks on handling the differences much more positively and leveraging those differences.

THE FOUR DICHOTOMIES

As per MBTI, there are four parameters that underline a person's personality type, in general. Each parameter has two dichotomies. The discussion below offers a simplified explanation of each type and dichotomy at work and is meant to be used as 'help guide' for young managers.

How People Energize at Work: Extroverts (E) versus Introverts (I)

As per MBTI, people generally prefer to get energized in two different ways. Either they receive energy from the outside world (called extroverts) or receive energy from the inside (called introverts, Table 5.1).

Extroverts: They are your colleagues with high energy. They are mostly known as 'people's person'. They like to work in groups, eat in groups and seek constant interactions. They enjoy others' attention. They want to network with their cohorts. Extroverts may be friends with a wide range of people, including colleagues outside their teams or projects.

Introverts: On the other hand, introverts are your colleagues who are quiet and do not prefer to talk a lot.

Table 5.1: How Do We Energize at Work

Extroverts (E)	Introverts (I)
Appealing characteristics:	Appealing characteristics:
Energetic; enthusiastic; may glue the team together; entertain and eliminate boredom; actively participate in activities; like to make presentations; like to pitch in their ideas	Deal with abstract ideas, memories, pictures, drawings quite well; think before they speak or act; clarity on their acts and plans; work behind the scenes often; do not seek validation or attention from cohorts; great focus or concentration
Off-putting characteristics:	Off-putting characteristics:
Too talkative; speak before they think; may not be taken seriously by others; jump into activities without giving much thought; may seem dominating; need attention; not let others speak during meetings or discussions; may get disappointed when not allowed to put forth ideas; may intimidate introverts with their energy levels; lacks focus	May come across as reserved or shy; get exhausted if job involves networking or attending unknown gatherings; may not pitch in ideas unless pushed to speak; may not have immediate answers to impromptu questions; may feel as a misfit in the team or group they are part of; difficult to multitask

Source: The author.

They are introspective and mostly immersed in their thoughts. They are self-contained and are less dependent on others, unless there is a work requirement. They prefer works that do not involve much interaction with colleagues. They focus on their tasks better

MASTERING BEHAVIOUR

when they are alone and prefer not to be disturbed. You would find them being part of smaller groups. They usually do not mingle with many people at work, hence, can be identified as loners. They prefer to talk less in the discussions or meetings too.

How People Collect Information: Sensing (S) versus Intuiting (N)

MBTI established that people could be differentiated based on the way they receive information from their surroundings. People are either sensors or intuitors (Table 5.2).

Sensors (S): Sensors are your colleagues who believe what they see. They trust their senses. They prefer information that is current and real. They focus on details that are specifically important to them. They are practical when it comes to receiving information from their surroundings.

Intuitors (N): Intuitors are the ones who notice abstract and creative ideas. They mostly explore the possibilities beyond what is evident. They remember impressions more easily than facts or details.

How People Evaluate Information and Take Decisions: Thinkers (T) versus Feelers (F)

MBTI categorizes people based on their methods of assessing information and making decisions (Table 5.3).

Thinkers (T): Your thinking colleagues prefer looking at data, information, objective standards and rationales. They make their decisions based on reasoning and logic to handle problems.

Table 5.2: How Do We Take Information

Sensing (S)	Intuiting (N)
Appealing characteristics:	Appealing characteristics:
Pay attention to evidence or physical reality; notice details; trust actual experiences; learning happens when they can put it to use; believe in experiences of self and others; follow what they see; focus on established steps and instructions	Pay attention to impressions or pattern parts of the information; like to visualize than wait for the hands-on experience; focus on the creative aspects and things that are not obvious; notice unique properties of the information; inventive; think about future implications than the past; excited about changes; read between the lines
Off-putting characteristics:	Off-putting characteristics:
Do not rely on information that is not explicit; only trust information in the form of evidence or experience; lack creative mind; cannot relate with abstract ideas; get too myopic and miss out on seeing the bigger picture; lost without instructions; cannot trust or understand symbols; challenging to connect dots when the information is haphazard and abstract; pay extra attention to facts, either present or past, that they are lost or disoriented without it in hand	Do not rely on information based on evidence as they trust their intuition more than anything else; explore new possibilities so much that miss out on reality; do not follow what they see; trust symbols or impressions too much; read too much between the lines

Source: The author.

MASTERING BEHAVIOUR

Table 5.3: How Do We Take Decisions

Thinking (T)	Feeling (F)
<u>Appealing characteristics:</u>	<u>Appealing characteristics:</u>
Weigh pros and cons while making decisions; like consistency and logic; impersonal in decision-making; prefer scientific explanations where logic is important; notice and point out inconsistencies; insist on making fair decisions; like to debate in order to seek logics; convinced by rational arguments	See how the decision impacts its stakeholders; establish harmony; involve emotions in decision-making; consider point-of-view of others involved; concerned about maximizing the benefit of people or community at large involved
<u>Off-putting characteristics:</u>	<u>Off-putting characteristics:</u>
Emotions go unnoticed while making decisions; come across as rude or dominating; can be perceived as argumentative; might unknowingly hurt feelers with their debates; direct and unable to be politically correct	Make biased decisions; might come across as manipulative; not able to be straightforward or direct as they are afraid of hurting others; get confused easily; get anxious when harmony is missing in decision-making; avoid the hard reality of the situation; may come across as people pleaser

Source: The author.

Feelers (F): If they prefer balancing their personal values or emotions while making decisions, they are feelers. While taking any decision, feelers attempt to establish harmony and make sure the decision does not hurt others.

General Orientation towards Life: Judgers (J) versus Perceivers (P)

The last category of dichotomy defines people's approach towards the world (Table 5.4).

Judgers (J): These are your colleagues who like to work in a defined and structured environment. They enjoy an orderly way of working. They are the ones who take their work quite seriously and sincerely.

Perceivers (P): Your colleagues who like to go with the flow are the perceiver types. They want to keep things open-ended and work spontaneously instead of pre-planning.

Table 5.4: How Do We Approach Life in General

Judging (J)	Perceiving (P)
Appealing characteristics:	Appealing characteristics:
Find comfort in planning and routine; prefer to keep things around them organized; like to follow the order of others; like to settle things; take the responsibilities very seriously; find comfort in	Find comfort in keep things flexible and open-ended; do not take deadlines so seriously; prefer spontaneity instead of routines; find comfort when allowed to go with the flow; do not involve much planning;

Judging (J)	Perceiving (P)
making 'to-do' list; take deadlines seriously; do not wait till the last moment to finish the assigned tasks; complete work on time; show up in the meetings on time and prefer that for others; like rules and want everyone to follow them	take things easy; prefer freedom to make things moving; like to incorporate new information till the last moment; comfortable with last-minute changes; do not get anxious when planning does not work out
Off-putting characteristics:	Off-putting characteristics:
Get anxious and nervous when things are not under control; freak out in uncertainties; take deadlines so seriously that they get under pressure with last-minute changes; take instructions so seriously that they come across as inflexible to others; come across as serious; work first, play later; sometimes, they focus so much on completing the task that they miss new information or needs for last-minute changes	Get anxious with a lot of rules and orders; question existing rules and its necessity; many times, deviate from what is expected; might be perceived as laid back or indifferent; seem untrustworthy because of casual attitude; miss out on deadlines; show up late a lot of time; play first, work comes later; at times, they miss making decisions on time

Source: The author.

IS THAT IT?

What we see in this chapter is a simplified explanation of MBTI specifically meant for first-time managers. The idea is to incorporate the understanding of the application of MBTI. In reality, MBTI is much broader. Not only you understand preferences on dichotomies, MBTI also offers 16 personality types based on these dichotomies. For example, you can be an extroversion (E), intuition (N), thinking (T), perception (P); introversion (I), intuition (N), feeling (F), judgement (J); introversion (I), sensing (S), feeling (F), perception (P); extroversion (E), sensing (S), thinking (T), judgement (J); etc.[3]

CAN PEOPLE HAVE A MIX OF BOTH DICHOTOMIES, AND WHAT DOES IT MEAN?

Yes. You may find your colleague comfortable with both abstract ideas and facts and numbers while processing information. Or a colleague is as good a performer when works in routine and order and in an unstructured environment. People with strong preferences of either side of dichotomy have more difficulty in switching preferences than people with similar preferences on both sides of the dichotomy. On the flip side, they might come across as inscrutable, manipulative and confused about situations. For example, in the words of Madhushree, a young manager, who has equal preferences on thinking and feeling, 'It is tough to choose between the available options because in a certain set of situations, I prefer something, and in other situations, I prefer something else. I generally go with the majority votes in such situations.'

---

[3] To know more in detail, you may refer to https://www.myersbriggs. org/my-mbti-personality-type/mbti-basics/

WHY SHOULD I KNOW ABOUT MY PEERS?

As a new employee, you want to experience more positive experiences with colleagues than bitter ones. That is the best way to channelize your energy in performing effectively instead of resolving conflicts. In a recent conversation, a young manager and my ex-student (who, by the way, is an introvert) mentioned to me, 'I have realized extroverts are an overconfident bunch of people. They overpower the groups and are way too aggressive in expressing their thoughts.' In another conversation, Guru, an introvert and a young manager, said, 'I do not take extroverts seriously. Every time we have a kick-off meeting, extroverts talk non-stop, mostly about things that are not relevant or related to the main point of discussion. We conduct meetings to brainstorm, not to chit-chat about nonsensical stuff. I would like my extrovert teammates to stick to the point and save us some time.'

To keep the relationships smooth and explore further opportunities to strike friendly conversations, you must first understand them and their preferences. Unless you know why they are behaving in a certain manner, it will be difficult for you to relate with them or their situations. MBTI offers a wonderful opportunity to better understand your colleagues and empathize with them instead of judging them. Moreover, MBTI enhances your empathy and compassion towards others. What more do you want as a new manager?

APPLICATIONS OF MBTI FOR FIRST-TIME MANAGERS

MBTI is an excellent tool for managers. New joiners can benefit from it the most if they understand it thoroughly.

While the application is quite broad, in the below section, we shall discuss the ones that will take you a long way at your workplace. Some of them include the following.

UNDERSTANDING YOUR COLLEAGUES' WORKING STYLES

The most fundamental application of the MBTI framework is understanding and familiarizing yourself with your teammates', boss's or clients' working styles. Irrespective of the organization you work for, the fact that all your team members are new and unfamiliar remains the same. You are required to gel well with them and bring things to the table collectively. You cannot afford to wait for the 'right time', make friends with them and develop close relationships. How will you manage your initial months working with them? You definitely do not want to get into unnecessary arguments and debates. One way in which MBTI can help you in such situations is giving you explanations on why 'X is behaving in a certain way'. As narrated by Bhargava, 'I am an introvert. I normally do not disclose my issues to many people. I express myself only to the closest ones at work. That creates many misunderstandings. For example, recently, I had a heated argument with a client for no serious reason. I did not mention it to my teammates. They still think I do not want to work with the client out of my laziness.'

A teammate who is continuously pushing you on the deadline without paying much heed to the fact that you had arrived only 15 days ago in the city and are perhaps arranging resources for yourself is definitely a pain in the neck. You may have not even settled in properly. What would you think about this person? I am sure you will sulk inside thinking why you have such a teammate in the first place. Isn't it? Though you do not know this person properly, it is safe to assume that they might be a 'judger' who gets anxious if things do not move on time. Maybe they are afraid of last-minute changes or missing deadlines. So, the idea is not to bother you but to get things moving without much ado.

FORMING IMPRESSIONS

Being new at work, no doubt, is full of challenges. The expectations of your colleagues are relatively high at the same time. Every time you pitch in your ideas, all eyes automatically fall on you. MBTI can help you form better impressions in front of others and drive them to build positive perceptions about you in little time.

Imagine it is your first boardroom presentation in front of your boss. While you know it will take you a while to learn the ropes, you try to give your best shot. You happen to be an 'intuitor' and like seeing bigger pictures. On the other hand, your boss is a sensor and relates with data, numbers, reality and what is present. You have been observing your boss for quite some time, and you have realized that talking about abstract information is not going to fetch you any appreciation. You plan your presentation accordingly. You consciously take your boss through the facts, figures and information that involves people's past experiences and how this idea was a success. Your boss, being a sensor, immediately connects with your thoughts. And there you go! You have successfully implanted a positive image of yourself in your boss's eyes. At the beginning of your career, you are expected to focus on 'what they want'.

Hence, utilize information about them and plan it accordingly to receive more appreciation for your work.

PERSUADING OTHERS

You are in a situation where you must convince your boss and boss's boss about the need to start a new IT project. Unless you get a green flag from both, you will not be allowed to initiate the project. You know that your boss is a thinker while their boss is a feeler. Can we convince both thinkers and feelers on the same set of information? Well, yeah. Try this trick. When you convince your boss, who is a 'thinker', highlight the project's pros and cons in terms of profit-loss or breakeven. You may choose to talk about a logical framework or an objective criterion based on which you feel the project is profitable to the unit. Your boss's boss, on the other hand, is a 'feeler'. Talking about logic and giving rationales on the utility of the project might not sound convincing to him/her. Figure out what is close to his/her heart. Revolve your arguments around that. To give you an example, you may convince the boss on the project by mentioning how it will impact the society at large. Or how this project will fulfil the vison of the ex-head of the department who is no more. You may also bring in the discussion about its impact on the stakeholders or the people involved in the decision. Follow the tip and see things working in your favour.

STRIKING FRUITFUL CONVERSATIONS

MBTI framework is quite helpful when it comes to building healthy and smooth conversations with colleagues. While it might take time for you to develop meaningful

MASTERING BEHAVIOUR

connections with them, you still have a chance to be socially more aware of your surroundings and not talk about things that cause them discomforts. To give you some tips, while talking with 'extroverts', show enthusiasm and energy. Talking with 'introverts' can be a bit tricky at times. Think through before you speak. Do not expect an immediate response to your queries. Allow them time to reflect and come back to you. As much as possible, communicate in writing instead of doing it verbally. With 'sensors', always focus on information. 'Intuitors' should be given creative space. They should not be asked to jump to the finish line or produce immediate output. They need to explore and think. While talking with 'thinkers', focus on primary issue and solutions. Use principles and rational behind your talks. 'Feelers' like recognition for the work they have done. Maybe a pat on the back would do too. Appreciate them for even smaller work. Show empathy. Ask them how they feel. 'Judgers' should be appreciated for their sincerity in completing the task. Do not talk about rules with 'perceivers'. Moreover, they should be allowed to be spontaneous.

LEVERAGING COMPLEMENTARY SKILLS

Most of the tasks at the managerial level of the hierarchy are interdependent on team members. As a new manager, you will be expected to work in teams. Your assigned tasks could be sequential (Y's task is dependent on X's), pooled (X and Y work together to complete a task) or reciprocal[4] (X and Y are sequentially dependent as well as reciprocally, on each other), depending on your project requirements.

---

[4] https://hbr.org/2017/03/is-your-team-coordinating-too-much-or-not-enough#:~:text=Because%20the%20type%20of%20coordination,pooled%2C%20sequential%2C%20and%20reciprocal

But do not panic if you think you are not quite a 'team player'. To simplify, if you are an extrovert but your teammate is an introvert, do not see this as an issue. It is not really a bottleneck, in case you thought so. Consider it a complimentary skill and utilize it to maximizing the benefits of your team.

A team that is a blend of different types of preference (say a mix of introverts and extroverts) is more resourceful than a homogenous group of purely extroverts or introverts. To give you an example, tasks that require networking, presenting, pitching ideas, persuading people, workshop visits, etc., can be given to 'extroverts'. Tasks that require thinking or generating ideas, writing, less talking, working in a small group of people can be easily allotted to the 'introverts'.

DELEGATING TASKS AND GETTING THE WORK DONE EASILY

Just as explained in the previous point, utilize skillsets of sensors, intuitors, judgers, etc., in the right kinds of tasks. This will not only save time but also would not put peers under unnecessary discomfort or pressure.

Here Maria, another one of my former students, shares her experience. 'In my first few months in the new job, I was asked to assist a client on a greenfield project. Imagine the difficulty! I am a judger. I need structures. I am not that person who will use spontaneity to perform tasks. I used to scratch my head daily on how to even begin the project from scratch. My performance was going down day by day, and anxiety levels were rising.'

On the other hand, a young manager, Amy shares, 'I was recently working on a very innovative project that we had started from scratch. While my team members were mostly following the standard procedure and exploring how competitors handled such projects in the past, being an intuitor, I was really looking to make the project fascinating and different, using my creative ideas. I did not have to put in a lot of efforts as it comes to me naturally. My work was really appreciated by the seniors later on.'

To resolve similar issues as discussed by Maria, ask your subordinates a few questions, and you will know their preferences to an extent.

> Do last-minute changes bother you? (If yes, they are judgers).
>
> Given a chance, how would you like to spend your free time? (Introverts/extroverts)
>
> What do you do if planning does not work out? (Judgers/perceivers)
>
> Do you want to make everyone around you happy with your decisions, or do you find difficult to make important decisions? (Feeler)

These are some of the quick questions to understand the working style of people and their preferences. People who are pretty serious about deadlines should be given ad hoc tasks more often. People who want to satisfy the needs of everyone around them should not be asked to make difficult decisions. People who do not like to socialize a lot should not be bombarded with tasks that involve networking or participating in unknown gatherings. Not that they cannot perform the required tasks. The fact is they can very well do the task even if it is not their preference. However, this will put them in a state of exhaustion. Such tasks will consume more time, make people more conscious, require them to put extra effort and still compromise the outcome.

CAN MBTI IDENTIFY PERSON–ORGANIZATION FIT AS WELL?

Read the following narrative by Ravi.

'I was working with XXX, India's largest public bank, before doing an MBA. I was supposed to follow instructions in everything I did, even switching on/off the system. Every step there is guided by the rulebook, and you are strictly not supposed to deviate from it. This job was absolutely not in sync with who I am. The main reason for my leaving that job was extreme dissatisfaction. I could not do anything creative. There was no independence. Even if I had great ideas, there was no scope to put that through the organization.'

Ravi happens to be an intuitor and a perceiver. The kind of organization he was part of and the work he was doing were not coherent with his preferred type of work. A person like Ravi is best suited for the organizations which are not driven by standard operating procedures. He is best fit for organization who are organic in nature, flexible, have space for creativity and spontaneity. Hence, in his case, we can clearly see a person–organization misfit.

In another example, Sourabh explains his plight.

MASTERING BEHAVIOUR

'Initially, I was working with a tech start-up. Being in a start-up, my main job was to develop new ideas for new projects, try new things and explore new methods of approaching issues. I was delighted to work in this set-up. The issue happened when my parents forced me to join the family business. It is a 20-year-old venture. They have established a way of doing things. The culture of following routine is deeply ingrained. I used to implement a lot of new ideas initially. But then, people were quite resistant to change. I was later on told to follow the routine instead of experimenting with things.'

Sourabh's preferred working style is precisely like Ravi's. By now, I am sure you have got an idea that this is another classic case of person–organization misfit. Note that just like we have a preferred way of working and have certain personality types, organizations too carry preferences and personalities. For example, some organizations interact with the outside world more often than the others (extroverts). Some organizations are more standardized and follow a routine (sensing), while others are creative and inventive (intuitive). Some organizations are more rational and focus on profit–loss or objective criterion while making important decisions (thinking), while others consider the community at large (feeling). Try seeking a fit and congruence between your preferred way of working and that of the organization. The better the fit, the better will be your career progression and well-being. We do not want to be in the position of Ravi or Sourabh after all!

SELF-REFECTION IS IMPORTANT TOO

As mentioned previously, unless you understand yourself and know how to lead yourself, there is no way you will learn how to understand, manage and lead others. MBTI not just offers you a wide gamut of possibilities to enhance your workplace interactions, it also gives you a chance to know yourself better. MBTI offers you answers to many questions you have been wondering about yourself so far. For example, what kind of job is fit for you, why you make individual decisions, your preferred way of living, your likes and dislikes, your biggest pet peeves, etc., can be explained using MBTI. So, before applying the discussed framework to others, apply it to yourself. Start observing your working styles. The more you know yourself, the better it will be to keep a check and control of your actions. As a new manager, the more you introspect, the better are the chances of self-improvement.

Q: How do I measure and assess MBTI scores?

A: There are majorly two ways in which you can assess your own or your colleagues' preferences on these four dichotomies. One way of knowing it is by taking an MBTI test to get accurate scores and understand your preferred type. Many online services can get you your scores for free.[5] Obviously, you cannot push them to fill a survey informally (you do not want to come across as a nagging, awkward colleague!). The other way of understanding the types is by making observations. Since you are new to the workplace, you have only a handful of information about your colleagues. Do notice their patterns of behaviours at various occasions, including corridor talks, boardroom presentations, kick-off meetings, one-on-one discussions, their thought process, way of communicating, etc. You will get a fair idea of their preferences.

Q: How is MBTI different from the previously discussed Big Five personality framework?

A: Do not get confused between these two frameworks. Though they both are personality frameworks, they are mutually exhaustive, that is, there are no overlaps. The first and foremost difference between MBTI and Big Five is while Big Five framework assesses your traits (long enduring, stable patterns

---

[5] For example, https://www.123test.com/jung-personality-test/; https://www.truity.com/test/type-finder-personality-test-new

of behaviours), MBTI simply assesses your personality type. That means MBTI identifies your preferred type in a given situation.

Since the Big Five personality framework assesses your traits, your scores tend to last longer. That means your scores would not change in the long run, unless you are exposed to severities of situations. MBTI scores, on the other hand, tend to change with situations. For example, when in college, you may have your MBTI scores consistent throughout, but they may change once you take up a job. Similarly, your MBTI scores may change from one job to another if the jobs' overall context is different from each other.

Given the different nature of these two frameworks, the utility of each of these are significant in different set of contexts. You may rely on the MBTI framework when exploring the types of the self or others. You may utilize the information (based on MBTI) in broader contexts such as managing conflicts, establishing connections, creating impressions, developing of the self and/or teams at work. The Big Five has predictive validity to job performance, which means your Big Five scores can predict your future job performance. They are also useful in predicting the fit between people and jobs. Besides, do not get confused between the definitions of extrovert/introvert in both models. If you noticed carefully, the explanation of these two facets in MBTI is much broader than that in the Big Five.

✳ 6 ✳

BELIEVE YOU CAN,
AND YOU'RE HALFWAY THERE

In an interview,[1] when Jack Welch was asked the explanation of effective organization, he said,

> For a large organization to be effective, it must be simple. For a large organization to be simple, its people must have self-confidence and intellectual self-assurance. Insecure managers create complexity. Frightened, nervous managers use thick, convoluted planning books and busy slides filled with everything they have known since childhood. Real leaders do not need clutter. People must have the self-confidence to be clear, precise, to be sure that every person in their organization—highest to lowest—understands what the business is trying to achieve. But it is not easy. You cannot believe how hard it is for people to be simple, how much they fear being simple. They worry that if they are simple, people will think they are simpleminded. In reality, of course, it is just the reverse. Clear, tough-minded people are the most simple.

[1] https://hbr.org/1989/09/speed-simplicity-self-confidence-an-interview-with-jack-welch

While rare studies[2] have argued that less confident people are the most successful, most of the studies have created consensus on the fact that high self-confidence led to successful careers. Overconfidence may lead to hubris, inability to accepts criticisms and under confidence to insecurity. A balanced level of self-confidence is desired to be successful at work and life in general. Understanding that fine line is crucial. Confident employees are considered assets to workplaces. For example, 'Employers benefit from confident employees because they are more positive contributors, more productive, good motivators, and make great role models. Additionally, confident employees in customer-focused or sales positions directly contribute to brand perception.'[3]

FACTORS HINDERING YOUR SELF-CONFIDENCE

I am sure you are already familiar with the factors that impact your confidence negatively. This segment highlights some not-so-commonly-discussed psychological, well-researched mechanisms that might distort or ascend your level of confidence.

SELF-FULFILLING PROPHECY

An ex-student, Stuti, who is currently working with a large multinational company, recently shared her story. In her words,

---

[2] https://hbr.org/2012/07/less-confident-people-are-more-su
[3] https://www.kaplanprofessional.edu.au/blog/why-is-confidence-in-the-workplace-important-and-how-do-i-improve mine.

MASTERING BEHAVIOUR

I was repeatedly told by my first boss at my previous work-place that I would never ever crack any client deal. Cracking business deals for a rookie is not a cakewalk, I know that. But every fresher goes through it, not just me. I have been a bright student, you know. I have been reasonably good in everything, be it studies, sports, social work, etc. I used to be a confident person. Despite that, the constant nagging from my boss dipped my confidence for real. No doubt, initially, my job was difficult. I had difficulty in closing deals. But the constant discouragement from my boss led me to almost give up on even trying. My confidence was shattered. I had internalized his opinion to such an extent that it crushed my confidence. I have got appreciation from my colleagues in the past. I was known to be diligent. But here, even before the conversations with clients could start, I would shiver and tell myself that I cannot do this. I would just sit there, feeling like a waste. To be honest, I stopped making efforts both before the client meetings and at the very moment, to perform well. I guess I had somehow told myself that this is too big for me to crack.

The question here is, 'are the expectations of others about your behaviour self-fulfilling?[4] In simple words, do positive or negative expectations of others from you affect your behaviour positively or negatively? *Others* here could be your friends, parents, spouse, colleagues, bosses, clients, etc. Think about it. Has it ever happened that your parents' low expectations

---

[4] https://www.sciencedirect.com/topics/social-sciences/self-fulfilling-prophecy

actually led to bad outcomes? Some of us have strict parents who have frequently told us that we will perform poorly in exams, and we ended up flunking the exams.

On the other hand, despite being an average performer, some kids have parents who keep incredibly high expectations, expecting them to outshine everyone else in the class. Well, the kid ends up being one of the top performers in the class. In my own MBA classes, sections that I repeatedly told are better performers ended up getting better average scores than the other sections I taught. Could that be magic? Does it seem inexplicable? Well, no!

Think about the following scenario:

MASTERING BEHAVIOUR

There are five members in your team who work on similar projects. However, the boss feels that you are smarter than everyone else and that you should hit the highest target by the end of the financial year. The positive expectation of your boss changes their own behaviour. They start paying more attention to your work, give you more constructive feedback, provide you support and encouragement and offer you resources that will help you achieve better than others. Due to your boss's positive behaviour towards you, your belief in self changes positively too. You utilize all the resources and help offered by your boss and work to perform better than others. You ultimately end up outperforming everyone else in the team. In the end, your boss's belief (that you will perform the best in the group) is strengthened by the positive outcome you have shown.

This is called 'Pygmalion effect'! The Pygmalion effect indicates that higher expectations (and positive beliefs about someone) lead to better performance.

Well, there is also a negative side of self-fulling prophecy (someone's expectation leading to confirmation) too! Yes, you guessed it right. Negative expectations about someone affects their performance negatively. This is called the 'Golem effect'! The previously mentioned example of Stuti is nothing but a result of Golem effect. In her case, boss's negative expectation about Stuti altered his belief about her performance, due to which he, perhaps, paid less attention to her and did not support or offer any kind of encouragement.

He also did not help her overcome the initial hurdles in her job and made the job even more difficult for her by always poking her about his low expectations. These behaviours of the boss altogether generated a negative belief for herself in Stuti, owing to which her performance went down.

LOCUS OF CONTROL: INTERNAL VERSUS EXTERNAL

Are you the person who owns all the successes and failures? Do you believe you can take charge of the crests and troughs of your life? If yes, you have an 'internal locus of control', as mentioned in the chapter 'Avoiding Workplace Loneliness'. On the other hand, if you give credit to externalities such as luck and considers all the life events are beyond your control, you have an 'external locus of control'. Your locus of control defines your feelings towards the events, and whether related outcomes are within your control or outside. It captures whether individuals 'attribute the cause or control of events either to themselves or to the external environment'.[5]

Your locus of control impacts your level of confidence to a great extent. Imagine you are a sales manager who is responsible for cracking five business sales deal in a year. Either you think your hard work and skillsets will get you through the deals or you put it on your luck thinking, 'If I am lucky, I will crack the deals.' The former indicates your internal locus of control and the latter, external locus of control. In another scenario, you found yourself on the list of best performers of the year. You credited the success to your continuous efforts, focus and perseverance (internal locus). Alternatively, you thought the acknowledgment could be

[5] Spector, P. E. (1988). Development of the work locus of control scale. *Journal of Occupational Psychology*, 61(4), 335–340.

because your boss is a known guy in the organization and he would have pushed your name, or its sheer luck that your name popped up in the list (external locus).

The way you identify with your life events (internal or external) determines your confidence and belief in yourself, impacting your career success. Further, a high locus of control builds positive attitudes, behaviour and well-being in the workplace.[6]

ROLE OF SELF-CONFIDENCE IN ENHANCING CONNECTIONS WITH PEERS/CLIENTS

It is no surprise that self-confidence improves performance and does wonders in other aspects of life. One of the significant influences of positive self-confidence is on 'relationships with others'. Research over the years has established that high self-confidence is an important parameter in improving self-esteem (i.e., your evaluation of your own worth), which, in turn, helps improve interpersonal connections. According to a longitudinal study by American Psychological Association,[7] 'people's self-esteem may influence whether they are successful in initiating and maintaining relationships with romantic partners, friends,

---

[6] B. M. Galvin, A. E. Randel, B. J. Collins, and R. E. Johnson, 'Changing the Focus of Locus (of Control): A Targeted Review of the Locus of Control Literature and Agenda for Future Research,' *Journal of Organizational Behavior* 39, no. 7 (2018): 820–833.

[7] M. A. Harris, and U. Orth, 'The Link between Self-esteem and Social Relationships: A Meta-analysis of Longitudinal Studies,' *Journal of Personality and Social Psychology* 119, no. 6 (2019): 1459–1477

and co-workers and whether they have a strong or weak social support network.'

To give you an example, building better connections with colleagues involves investing your time and resources. Asking the help of colleagues, appreciating them on their achievements, extending support and helping them, raising your voice for them, etc., are some of the ways that help you strike closeness with colleagues. Suppose a scenario where both you and your teammate applied for a succession planning/promotion opportunity at work. It so turned out that due to better performance of the teammate, your colleague bagged that position. This event can highly demotivate you or make you feel inferior about yourself in case you possess low self-confidence.

On the contrary, if your self-confidence is high, you will retain self-belief even in adverse situations. Unless you are 'secure about yourself' and have faith in your abilities, you won't appreciate the achievement of your colleague. While you may congratulate the teammate and pretend to be happy, you will not be able to fully cope with this situation. You will keep sulking inside, and that would make your 'relationship bitter'. In fact, many times, you end up belittling them as you are not quite self-assured about your achievements. At times, your negative emotions come out explicitly to others, again putting you in a bad light at work.

Self-confidence also impacts your impression on peers or on clients. It may sound mean, but people who have shaky confidence are not taken seriously, especially in workplace contexts. In the words of my ex-student Bhawna, who comes across as intelligent and a confident sales executive,

146

'Every time I prepare to meet my clients, I make sure I come across as a confident person. I dress up nice, do my pre-preparations well and make sure my body language is all professional. I feel the days I am not feeling good about myself, somehow, it reflects on my face. My confidence helps me make my client willing to listen to my ideas.'

Not just people take you more seriously when you come across as a confident personality, 'they also value you' and your presence around them. There is an automatic aura that confident people create with their presence. You might not know everything, you might not have a grasp over all the topics, but a confident 'I don't know' is better than an answer spoken with shaky confidence. People want to talk more and listen to those who have a positive aura, who have faith in themselves and who share their failure stories full of self-belief. Ask yourself, 'would you want to hang out often with those who come across as confident people with a sense of self-respect or those who have shaky confidence and are self-deprecating all the time?'

Another aspect to consider is 'your belief in the self, impacts your beliefs in others'. A confident person evaluates people and their surrounding positively. Unless you believe in your abilities, you will not show confidence in others and their abilities. No one can really 'learn' from you if you are not a secure person. With positive self-beliefs, you may set a benchmark for others and, in fact, guide them to 'own up' their success and failures. This will further help you make more friends at work. Your teammates and subordinates will like you for who you are and the inspiration they get from you; now that is a bonus, ain't it? I am sure you get the point I am trying to make. Hence, all in all, your level of confidence says a lot about your satisfaction with the interpersonal relationships you have.

IMPROVING SELF-CONFIDENCE: NOT A BARRIER ANYMORE!

You have been in this job for a few months. You realize everything you do is new; basically, you are a rookie! Every time you get a new project in hand, you ask yourself, 'Will I be able to do it?' Every new task that your boss gives you makes you nervous. Moreover, you often sneak a peek at other new joinees to see if they are equally hesitant in performing the same task. You set an expectation for yourself, positive or negative. Every time I was given challenging (and new) projects in my initial career, I had been in self-doubts. I, too, have asked myself, 'What if I fail?' just like you did. What I realized is that every time I accept the project (even with low confidence), thinking I will do it, I have succeeded. But at times, when I was in constant fear of failing, I have performed poorly. This is nothing but your own self-fulfilling prophecy.

SET HIGH EXPECTATIONS AND BELIEFS FOR YOURSELF

The takeaway is always maintaining high expectations from self. Tell yourself, 'I am capable of doing it', 'I will manage to deal with the difficulties', 'I am sure this is not too difficult for me', 'There is a reason that I have been trusted with this work'. Once you have developed positive expectations for yourself, you would have formed positive beliefs about managing the assigned tasks without much worry. But the moment you begin the assigned tasks with low expectations of yourself, you let your self-beliefs to go down. Do not let thoughts such as 'I am not meant for this project', 'Why did they give me such work', 'I have never ever done it before' or 'I am too young to tackle such big responsibility' creep in your mind. Poor expectations from yourself will lead to poor self-beliefs, thereby affecting your performance badly.

INHALE CONFIDENCE, EXHALE SELF-DOUBT

In practicality, it is not always possible to take charge of everything happening in your life. There are trying times when things go beyond your control. But always remember, your perceptions about yourself impact your attitude and, therefore, behaviour. Hence, your perceptions about yourself matter more than reality. If you have an internal locus of control, you need not worry. You have positive self-beliefs. By chance, if you are the one with an external locus of control, you might have shaken self-belief and, therefore, low self-confidence. Start creating positive perceptions about self. Take charge of your life events and their outcomes. Own your failures as much as you own your successes. If you succeed, give a pat on your back. Tell yourself you did well. Acknowledge your success and reward yourself. Appreciate and recognize your efforts too.

On the other hand, if you are met with failures, own them equally with a positive spirit. Do not think it happened because of the environment, bad luck, another person or their actions. Figure out the reasons for the failure within the self, as much as possible.

Note that I am not saying always 'blame' yourself for your failures! You need not be self-deprecating all the time. But try cultivating an internal locus of control by 'choosing' what you want in life and taking charge of events in your life. You must accept your failures with a positive spirit. Tell yourself you did not do as per the expectation this time, but you will do better next time. You 'chose' not to work hard enough to get the promotion, or you did not really 'want' a pay raise that desperately; hence, you did not put enough effort in that direction.

CAREFULLY CHOOSE WHO YOUR INSPIRATION IS

Imagine your goal is to lose weight. You are impressed seeing the toned physic of Bollywood actress Katrina Kaif. You closely start following her workout routine, her daily diet, etc. But you cannot really follow this forever. Or shall I say, it is not easy for you to relate with the actress's life for long as you two live in different space altogether? Instead, follow people who share the same journey as yours and have achieved significance in life. For example, as a young manager, you dream of becoming a chief experience officer of your company one day. Following your senior who has come from the same middle-class background, with similar struggles, and has achieved top position in your company will help you give a better direction than following, say, Elon Musk's journey.

Another critical thing to note here is 'encouraging appreciation'. You would not find anybody who does not like appreciation, acknowledgment and/or recognition from others. Recall in school how much you liked it when your teacher complimented you in front of the entire class. You used to get butterflies in the stomach. You used to repeat similar tasks (be it helping another student, getting high scores in your tests or even helping your teacher carry her copies to the staff room) to receive more praises. That used to impact your confidence hugely. The validation from others is intact in humans, irrespective of their age. Seek out activities that get you valuable and significant recognition from colleagues.

Further, note that just like you, everybody else loves appreciation. Do not leave an opportunity to appreciate others for their work or the efforts they are putting in. Even small compliments do wonders in making others happy. This works in a feedback loop. The more you notice little things others do and compliment them, the more they make a point to appreciate you. It will cost you nothing, and the returns are immense. Needless to say, it makes a lot of impact in improving the quality of your relationships. In the words of Mark Twain, 'I can live for two months on a good compliment.'

A FEW 'NOT-SO TALKED ABOUT' THINGS THAT YOU MAY FOLLOW

I will quickly come to the main point here. I am sure you have googled 'how to improve confidence' for yourself or for a friend at least once in life. There are umpteen articles that talk about 'building confidence'. I can bet they are relevant and have helped you in some way or the other. In this section, I have a few suggestions to offer (mostly the uncommon ones), based on my own experience and that of my interviewees.

1. *Keep a check of your emotions and mental health*: They help create a 'feel-good' attitude about yourself. Days on which you do not really feel positive about yourself or life in general, do not force yourself to get

into essential tasks wherein confidence is necessary. Be light on yourself.

2. *Learn to value yourself*: Unless you value yourself, no one else will value you. You do not need to be the best performer of your business unit for this. You should value your worth even if you do not have as big achievements as someone else in a particular domain. Remember that everyone has a different success story.

3. *Observe things that build your confidence*: Try to incorporate those in your day-to-day life. For some, big achievement does the work. For others, things such as dressing up well, good communication, impressive body language or an excellent work presentation matter.

4. *Own up your failures as confidently as you own up your success*: Maintain internal locus of control as much as possible. Recall the discussion we have had at the beginning of this chapter.

5. *Prepare*: There are some events when you need to showcase your confidence much more than regular days. Preparation is everything. For example, if you have a stage or a boardroom presentation, prepare an hour's worth of content for a half an hour presentation. A list of primary and secondary 'pointers to speak' helps in this regard.

6. *Accepting your fears is a good start*: Unless you do not accept what makes you anxious, you will not push your boundaries to pursue difficult tasks. Once you confront what scares you or makes you feel low about yourself, you know you need to work on it and hone your skills in that direction. For example,

MASTERING BEHAVIOUR

if speaking in the meetings scares you, accept it. Tell yourself you will try to improve. Make it a point to talk in meetings even if you do not have substantial points to contribute.

7. *Say no to saying no*: Do not always say *no* to difficult tasks or the tasks you have not done earlier. Take it as a challenge or consider it as an opportunity to grow and learn. While it is true that some tasks require more preparation and expertise than others, trust that it can be known and improved over time.

8. *Either be less critical or use it as your driver to motivation*: Some of us are overcritical about ourselves. What that means is we pay too much attention or over analyse our activities than that of others. For example, when you watch a recorded video of your presentation, you focus more on the mistakes you made while speaking. But when you watch others talking, you always focus on their content and do not critically analyse their speech flaws. If you are too self-critical, use this habit as a source of motivation to improve yourself instead of criticizing over and over.

9. *Celebrate small achievements*: Set for yourself small, a little challenging but realistic goals. Reward yourself every time you accomplish something. Be proud of your achievements. Achieving something does not necessarily include meeting your sales target or receiving the highest performance rating. Helping a colleague in his/her crucial time or guiding a subordinate to make better presentations counts as an achievement. Make a record of it and remind yourself about it from time to time.

10. *Promise less, deliver more*: Imagine a scenario where you delivered more than you promised to your boss. Even though you feel you are capable of doing more, keep it low-key. Do not showcase all your skills in one go. Showcase your talent, one at a time. Always promise to deliver less than what you can do and then put your best efforts to outperform yourself. Nothing gives more kick and an adrenaline rush than being an over-achiever at work.

11. *Ask questions*: For a new manager, it is inevitable to feel dumb, less competent, and incapable of performing specific jobs. Note that not just you, all your contemporaries out there may feel deadlocked initially or at some point of career. Understand that if you feel ambiguous about certain tasks, do not hesitate to ask questions or clarifications. Moreover, no question is a dumb question. The more you simplify things for you, the easier it will be for you to understand and perform. If you do not ask questions, you will get into a vicious loop of confusion, making yourself feel less about your competencies and knowledge.

ATTENTION: YOU MIGHT FALL INTO THE TRAP OF 'LEARNED HELPLESSNESS'

Have you ever fallen to certain situations where you accepted your defeat thinking 'I cannot resolve this situation ever' or 'This is how it is. I should accept it'? Beware, it's a trap that your brain is tricking you! Well, don't get me wrong. I am referring the situation as a 'trap' as there are possible ways to get out of learned helplessness even before it starts bugging you and getting over you. Imagine a situation wherein every time your boss had asked you to work on a statistics of data, you performed poorly. Repeated fear of performing poorly in statistics has scared you. Now, whenever you are presented with statistics, you feel you cannot perform. Even when an opportunity to fix the situation comes up, you do not try, assuming you will fail to perform anyway. This is a state called learned helplessness.

According to Macmillan (2018),[8]

> When people face a situation they don't like, most common response is to try to do something to make things better. However, if they find that they have little control over what happens, they may simply stop trying. This is called learned helplessness. This decision, to accept aversive circumstances, may hold even when it becomes possible to actually change things. For example, imagine a workplace where employees are unhappy about the way the work is distributed. The employees complain to their boss and even to human resource manager, and although the people in power may agree with the employees, nothing ever changes. Over time, the employees who stay with the job learn to accept the poor conditions.

Note that the ongoing feeling of learned helplessness severely impacts our emotional, cognitive and behavioural

---

[8] https://hbsp.harvard.edu/product/W18651-PDF ENG?Ntt=Learned +helplessness&itemFindingMethod=Searchh

outcomes. It creates sense of anxiety and depressive symptoms. Instead of accepting that there is no way you can resolve the situation or come out of it, start developing confidence to work on solutions. In fact, do not let the situation become repeatedly uncomfortable for yourself. Nip it in the bud by working on solutions without complaining about the difficulty of the situation.

BOOSTING THE CONFIDENCE OF YOUR COLLEAGUES: WHY NOT?

Apart from the suggestions mentioned above to improve your own confidence, you may want to help your peers develop their confidence. Just like you have struggled in your job, others may have too. But now you know the mechanism through which you can support your peers or juniors in enhancing their self-confidence. Just like your boss's high expectations from you positively impact your performance, setting positive and high expectations for others will surely impact their performance, hence, helping them build their self-confidence.

To give you an instance, a young woman (a postgraduate in psychology) joined me to assist in my academic affairs and research projects. This was her first stint with any IIM. Needless to say, her confidence was relatively low since the beginning, probably because of all the stories she had heard from her colleagues. In every small and big project I assigned to her, she made mistakes. I kept highlighting her errors and she kept making more mistakes. It became a vicious cycle. The situation became worse towards the end of the year. During her performance appraisals, her ratings went down, and she was put on a warning period

MASTERING BEHAVIOUR

for three months. This was the time I called her for one-on-one interaction. I inquired about her issues and told her to frankly share the challenges she has been facing in the job. In her words, 'I am not capable of performing research tasks. I have never done it. Plus, I think I am not meant for this position. I am not confident enough to face such an audience in the class on a daily basis.'

I felt bad, though I did not have much help to offer. I had three months to make changes in her behaviour in whatever way I could do. I leveraged the understanding of the Pygmalion effect. I started giving her more difficult projects and made her believe she can do it. I kept telling her things such as 'I think you are the best person to do this task', 'I know it is beyond the purview of your work, but you try it once. I am sure you will succeed' and 'Only you can help me complete this task'. And it worked! She gave her best performance in those three months. I was surprised, but I knew it was explainable. I started setting high expectations for her, I started spending more time grooming her on her communication, email writing, public speaking, helping with small research activities. This improved her self-belief and she ended up being more polished in the job.

FINALLY, KNOW YOUR CORE SELF-EVALUATIONS

While you should not settle for less in terms of your self-worth, you should not repeatedly beat yourself up to be the 'best' person out there. In the words of Gautam Buddha, 'You yourself, as much as anybody in the entire universe, deserve your love and affection.' Accept your strengths and flaws gracefully. If you possess low confidence in yourself, gradually work on the suggested areas and focus on building your core self-evaluations (CSEs). CSEs are your fundamental assessment of yourself and your environment. It is an aggregate of four sub-dimensions, that is, self-efficacy, self-esteem, locus of control and emotional stability. Here, generalized self-efficacy estimates one's fundamental ability to cope with a wide range of situations. Self-esteem is an overall assessment of one's self-worth, locus of control—the individual believes that people control events in their lives, and emotional stability is the tendency to feel secure.[9] Higher confidence automatically enhances your CSE. CSE is quite important for first-time managers and crucial in job success.

To understand your core self-evaluations (CSE),[10] ask yourself the following questions:

I am confident I get the success I deserve in life: Yes/No

I rarely feel depressed: Yes/No

When I try, I generally succeed: Yes/No

When I fail, I rarely feel worthless: Yes/No

I complete tasks successfully: Yes/No

I rarely feel that I am not in control of my work: Yes/No

Overall, I am satisfied with myself: Yes/No

I have confidence in my competence or ability: Yes/No

I determine what will happen in my life: Yes/No

[9] https://en.wikipedia.org/wiki/Core_self-evaluations

[10] T. A. Judge, A. Erez, J. E. Bono, and C. J. Thoresen, 'The Core Self-Evaluations Scale: Development of a Measure,' *Personnel Psychology* 56, no. 2 (2003): 303–331.

I feel that I am in control of my success in my career: Yes/No

I am capable of coping with most problems: Yes/No

Things rarely look bleak and hopeless to me: Yes/No

If most of your answers are affirmative, your fundamental evaluations about yourself and your environment are positive, which is a good indication. If you find half or most of the answers in 'No', you must work on suggestions given in this chapter and re-evaluate your CSE after a couple of months to check the positive changes in self. Note that confidence is not a disposition; that means it can be built up or improved. A series of consistent efforts in this regard will go a long way in your career.

Q: How do I keep my confidence up when I am continuously failing despite putting my best foot forward? Also, how do I keep up my confidence in general? For example, discussions in many office meetings are very general. Anyone can participate and put forward their opinion, but still, despite having an answer, I do not have the confidence to pitch in and respond. Is there any practice or solution which I can adopt to improve on this?

A: It is absolutely normal to lack self-confidence as it is one of the very common human psychology (to feel low about oneself at some point). Those who look confident to you now might have gone through it at one point.

Generally, it could occur because of many controllable or non-controllable factors such as childhood issues, bad experiences with classmates or teachers, unsuccessful relationships, poor academic grades, etc. It depends upon the fact whether it is a short-term issue or has been happening for a long while. All in all, any negative feeling tends to be associated with fear of something.

Apart from following the suggestions mentioned in the chapter, you should figure out what fear it is, and what is causing it. So, the point of discussion should be around overcoming that fear. Find the root cause, if possible. Once that is done, next step should be to tell yourself 'I am ready to face it today.' It will put you in a lot of anxiety on day one and two, but trust me, it would never bother you after that.

To give you an example, fear of spiders can be overcome by first explaining oneself what caused that fear (maybe when I was a child, a spider jumped on me, causing me discomfort). Second, telling yourself, 'It is just a spider; it cannot harm me', 'the size difference between the spider and me is huge', 'it is spider's instinct to crawl; not meant to scare me'. Third, once you have gained affirmation from your inner self, face a spider every time you encounter one. You might shiver at first, but the idea is to condition your brain with the thought that 'I am not afraid of it anymore.' Do try these three steps and see it working for you. Next time, just push yourself to participate in the meetings (right or wrong point, it does not matter; you must speak). By the third or fourth attempt, you will start feeling at ease. Remember, there is nothing we cannot conquer. It is all about how to train your brain.

ROLE OF FEEDBACK

Recently, in a conversation with Rithwik, my former student and now a successful senior manager in a manufacturing firm, he mentioned, 'As a team lead, I used to get deployed in high-risk projects; senior managers or group heads used to directly reach out to me regarding some of their other projects. I used to feel like a perfectionist. I was known for giving tough ratings and share the feedback upfront with my team members. Everything seemed cool; until one day, my subordinates were probed about my leadership qualities during leadership training. To my surprise, I was not rated positively on my leadership skills. All this while, what I had not realized was that my subordinates thought I was very politically connected and would harm their careers by reporting their mistakes to senior management. They were often reluctant to inform me about the issues or misses they may have made in their work. It was only through detailed reviews late in the project lifecycle that I would identify these misses and would need to spend double the time and effort to fix those issues late in the game. After the probing session, I discussed with the team and reiterated that I will never throw any of them 'under the bus'. I backed this with multiple instances where I took the blame for any misses and appreciated each individual's role in achieving key milestones publicly. This helped me gain the team's trust and build more honest and trustful relationships with the team.'

Many of us have sailed in the boat same as Rithwik. Many of us fear feedback from others, or we simply do not care; until some day, we come across experiences that appal us. This is not surprising, as feedback mostly indicates a slew of criticism. We are afraid to listen to others' comments on us as we do not like being judged. Fair enough. But then, ask yourself, 'Are you doing everything right?' 'Are you always correct?' 'Would you want to know their side of the story as well?' If yes, how often do you approach others to take their feedback? Are you rightly focusing on opportunities for self-improvement? Does your pursuit to enhance interpersonal relationships seem just one-sided? These questions might confuse some of us as we like to believe we are perfect in our little social worlds. And if not perfect, we rationalize things saying, 'I prefer being this way, like it or not,' and not pay much heed to what others say of us. Wise enough?

I am not sure! And naturally, when things do not work out, we end up accusing others for the fault. Remember, a bad carpenter always blames his tools. Recall all the discussions we have had in previous chapters. You might have the best of skills and competence, but it's of no use if you are not using them appropriately. And how do you decide if you are using them appropriately? You need to ask those who have been observing you and dealing with you on a day-to-day basis. Listening to their narratives about you, having mutual and open discussions with them and carefully listening and positively accepting what they have to say will make a huge difference in life.

Imagine a scenario wherein you visited a café with your partner, expecting to spend a great evening together. While the ambiance was outstanding, you and your partner did not like the food quality. Unless there is a corrective feedback mechanism for customers, how would the café manager know about the grievances and improvement areas? Seeking and accepting corrective feedback is an essential part of the learning process and should be practiced without hesitation.

Especially for first-time managers, feedback plays a crucial role.

In the words of Aamir, an HR consultant at a global firm, 'Taking feedback from others, I think, is the simplest yet most powerful method to understand people's perception about ourselves. My colleagues' positive perceptions about me helped to publicize my work among the leaders in my own experience. This happened as my colleagues with a positive perception about me advocated for me and, in a way, promoted me to my seniors. On the contrary, some of my colleagues did not have a particularly good opinion about me and my work. I never hesitated to directly reach out to them and ask for their feedback. Some of their comments have helped me a great deal in my work.'

Needless to say, professionals like Aamir have more growth opportunities at work owing to their ability to accept constructive feedback from peers.

ART OF BUILDING RELATIONSHIPS THROUGH FEEDBACK SOLICITATION

One of my recent conversations with my ex-student Rithika, who holds a mid-level position in an Indian manufacturing company, mentioned, 'Knowing what perception my manager has of me helps me understand myself better. Any constructive feedback my peers give me helps me mould myself accordingly. Though I do not believe in changing my principles and ideologies, I could change how I express or communicate with others. I do not want to be portrayed negatively; I do not want to get judged for wrong things. If I know what is running in their minds, it would be easy for me to control the situation. Further, it helps me smoothen the conversation.'

It goes without saying that everyone, just like Rithika, in their early careers or otherwise, seek others' support, be it one-on-one guidance and mentoring or through the feedback solicitation. In this regard, Johari window is a popular tool that aims at enhancing self-awareness and building relationships with others. Johari window allows us an opportunity to understand how and what others perceive of us. Especially for first-time managers, the Johari window is an effective tool for personal growth and establishing and maintaining relationships with peers.

The Johari window framework was established by two psychologists Joseph Luft and Harrington Ingham (hence, *JoHari*) in 1955 and has been in vogue since then. It mainly intends to improve our relationship with ourselves (by helping us know more about ourselves) and with others (by understanding others' points of view). It has been one of the most applied instruments in the areas of self-development, emotional intelligence, interpersonal relationships, dealing with conflicts, improving communications and so on in a workplace context. The psychologists explain,

> Like a happy centipede, many people get along
> fine working with each other, without worrying

166   **MASTERING BEHAVIOUR**

about which foot to put corrective feedback forward. But when there are difficulties, when the usual methods do not work, when we want to learn more-there is no alternative but to examine our own behavior in relation to others.[1]

DO YOU KNOW WHAT YOU DON'T KNOW? OVERCONFIDENCE AMONG BEGINNERS

While reading the previous chapters, you must have been wondering why we had discussed so much about self-awareness only to arrive at 'seeking feedback from others' at the end. While beginners or first-time managers are susceptible to be vulnerable and pessimistic, it is also established that they are overconfident about their abilities. According to a Harvard article, 'Beginners start off overconfident. They start a new task or job as "unconscious incompetents," not knowing what they do not know. Their inevitable early mistakes and miscues prompt them to become conscious of their shortcomings.'[2]

Knowing about 'Dunning–Kruger effect' in this regard is crucial for early managers. Dunning–Kruger's effect focuses on one's ignorance of being ignorant. It is a cognitive bias wherein the less competent think very highly of themselves and assume they know a lot. As defined by Dunning and

---

[1] J. Luft, and H. Ingham, 'The Johari Window: A Graphic Model of Awareness in Interpersonal Relations,' *Human Relations Training News* 5, no. 9 (1961): 6–7.

[2] As cited in https://hbsp.harvard.edu/product/H048R2-PDF-ENG? Ntt=dunning&itemFindingMethod=Search

Kruger, 'those who are incompetent, for lack of a better term, should have little insight into their incompetence'—an assertion that has come to be known as the Dunning–Kruger effect.[3] This cognitive bias has been explored a lot in self-assessments, performance management, skills and competence and learning, including other work fields.

Drawing from the above argument, it makes sense that your manager does not entirely rely on your self-assessment when it comes to your communication, competence or performance. A 360-degree view of oneself is as essential for early-managers as it is for the administrators/bosses. Hence, it may be safely assumed that, at the beginning of our career, we know little. But we are overconfident about abilities a lot of time. Therefore, while it is significant to understand the self from our own experiences, efforts and observations, it is crucial to involve feedback from others to give a wholesome narrative to the situations. That's when the role of taking input from others comes into play, especially when you are starting it all new.

SO, WHAT IS 'JOHARI WINDOW' ALL ABOUT?

Johari window offers a self-help four-quadrant framework that includes: open area, blind area, hidden area and unknown area (Figure 7.1).

---

[3] J. M. Kruger, and D. Dunning, 'Unskilled and Unaware of It: How Difficulties in Recognizing One's Own Incompetence Lead to Inflated Self-assessments, *Journal of Personality and Social Psychology* 77, no. 6 (1999): 1121–1134.

MASTERING BEHAVIOUR

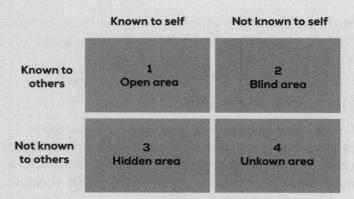

	Known to self	Not known to self
Known to others	1 Open area	2 Blind area
Not known to others	3 Hidden area	4 Unkown area

Figure 7.1: A Johari Window Framework

Source: The author.

QUADRANT I—OPEN AREA

Open area (aka arena) indicates the feelings, information, motivations or behaviours about you that are most open and transparent, that is, things about you and your behaviours are known to you and others. Johari's framework suggests open areas to be the most positive and essential for an individual's professional life. The best course of action is to maximize this window as much as possible.

Imagine a scenario where you joined organization X right after college. Indeed, you are unaware of your new surroundings. Your team members are unknown; the boss is new. But one thing that you are aware of is your own behaviour. Make a point that you keep yourself transparent with others. For example, Sameer is a jovial person who likes to crack jokes with everyone, including his own clients. If Sameer's clients are aware of him being jovial as much as Sameer knows about it, there would be better communication ease. Nobody will get hurt by taking the jokes personally.

Focusing on the open area helps to build better communication, trust and understanding between you and your colleagues.

QUADRANT II—BLIND AREA

This area indicates what is known to others about you is not known to you, that is, information about you and your behaviours that is not visible to you as of now. Johari's framework suggests reducing this area as much as doable. As explained by Joseph Luft (1982),

> To have all of me available to myself, I need your data about me. I need that part of my totality, my truth that you possess, my BLIND area. Why is it important to have the me that you have inside your head? Because what I believe about me is just that. A belief. It is not a reality until I exhibit specific behavior that defines me. To know if I exhibit any such behavior (do my actions show that I am honest, helpful, direct, sexist, callous, lazy?) I must have your 'experience-knowledge-experience' of me. What kind of person am I to you?

Every time Sameer makes an important presentation in front of his boss or other colleagues, he talks too loudly. He also makes errors due to a lack of preparation. Sameer does not realize these mistakes, and he feels the presentation had been flawless. However, the audience points out his mistakes, and he feels itched about them. The better scenario for Sameer would be to take feedback from the audience to understand certain behaviours that others observed, but he is not aware of them. Being receptive to corrective or constructive feedback will help Sameer grow as a professional.

Not just your colleagues, try reducing your blind area by taking 360-degree feedback with your direct and indirect stakeholders such as suppliers, clients, boss's boss and so on. In the words of a professional working for business-to-business sales for a firm, 'Our customers who do not have positive opinions about some of our sales representatives tend to not purchase company products from them. We have seen multiple times how negative perceptions about sales reps have spoiled the entire sales game. It is crucial to know why our clients feel in a certain way about those sales reps. Asking their concerns and understanding the reasons as to why they have formed perceptions is important in any client-facing job. If we underestimate clients' perception and not manage properly, the company may lose many customers in the long run. Hence, in jobs like ours, taking feedback from clients and customers is far-reaching.'

As per the Johari window, your blind area should be as small as possible. Asking for feedback from others will help you reduce your blind spot, thereby increasing your open area.

QUADRANT III—HIDDEN AREA

Hidden area indicates the undisclosed information, feelings, motivations and behaviours that you have kept hidden from others. You may possibly be hiding certain things about yourself from others due to the fear of judgement, rejection or disapproval from others or you may be driven to hide due to some ulterior motives. Therefore, a hidden area indicates things that you know about yourself but your colleagues don't. Rightly assumed, the hidden area must be reduced as much as possible, thereby increasing your open area.

Sameer has of late realized he is not enjoying office parties. Personal issues are going on at home with his spouse. He is trying to avoid weekend office parties as much as possible. Since Sameer is not significantly old in the organization, many people do not know him closely. Especially, his own team members are thinking that Sameer is purposely avoiding them. Had Sameer shared the actual issue or at least hinted why he is unable to enjoy office parties, the pre-conceived notions that his colleagues formed could have been averted, isn't it?

Therefore, one way in which hidden areas can be reduced is through self-disclosure. Note that while hidden area insists us to share important information about us as much as possible with others, it never says one must forcefully share information that may put them in a vulnerable situation later. For instance, in Sameer's case, it is okay to not share the actual issues going on at home with the spouse, but just hinting or making the colleagues aware that he cannot make it to the parties because of personal issues, though he wants to be part of it.

QUADRANT IV—UNKNOWN AREA

The unknown area is the most complex and unexplored one out of the four. This area indicates things that neither you know about yourself nor your colleagues know. Things that are deeply ingrained and are unconscious in nature mostly fall in this area. An unknown fear, aversion, inexplicable feeling of resistance, unspecified disorders, etc., fall in this area. Though it is not easy to reduce this area, self-discovery or shared discovery can help to some extent. This area does not have much significance for the detailed discussion in a workplace context. If unknown feelings bother you, the best course of action is to seek help of an expert such as a psychologist.

APPLYING JOHARI WINDOW IN THE WORKPLACE

Now, it is your turn to create a Johari window for yourself. First of all, choose at least four to five teammates or colleagues you are working with and wish to improve communication and relationships. Separately meet them and mention your intention to improve yourself and your relationships with the important stakeholders. Ask each of them to write at least three to five positive and negative things about you based on their observations about you and/or interactions with you. Meanwhile, write for yourself positive and negative things

that you know of yourself. Now, collate all the responses and create a Johari window (as mentioned in the below image) for yourself. In this regard, things that appear on both your and your colleagues' (one or more colleagues) lists, place it in the 'open quadrant'. If things appear on your list but not on the colleagues', place them in the 'hidden quadrant'. Last, things that appear on the colleagues' list but not yours, put them in the 'blind quadrant'.

For example, if one or more colleagues said I am selectively social, I would put it in an open area, as this information is out in the open and transparent and is known to me. If I said I am not a creative person but my colleague(s) mentioned that as my strength (they believe I am creative and that's my strength), it will go to my blind area. If I said good writing skills are my strength but my colleague(s) did not write that about me, this possibly is a hidden area. So far, I have not revealed my skills or have not indulged in activities where my writing skills could be showcased to others. Another scenario could be that even though I perceive myself to be a good writer, I am actually not, in eyes of the people I work with.

MY JOHARI WINDOW IS READY. WHAT NEXT?

I suggest you be open-minded and receptive when others offer their corrective feedback. In fact, at times, you might end up receiving destructive feedback (or feedback less helpful in nature). To avoid that, it is crucial for the person to know what this task is all about and what you are trying to achieve. In case you still receive things that impact you negatively or hurt you in any way, do not pay much heed to it. Count only those feedbacks that can improve you personally or professionally in some way. The rest of it is not essential. Discard that; they are not meant to be taken too seriously.

The next step is to sit with each of them and probe them to explain or reflect more on things they have said in the feedback. For example, if somebody mentioned you being short-tempered and that you need to work on it, ask them why they felt you are short-tempered, and if possible, probe them to share incidents when they felt so about you. This will offer you better clarity on things that you should work on. Also, ask them to offer suggestions. Ask them, had they been in your situation, how would've they have handled this situation? Do not hesitate to know more about yourself. Note that you only know part of your reality. The others contain at least some information about you. Through the Johari window exercise, our intention is to catch hold of the reality of you that is not known to you much. The reality that will help you grow as a better person and a professional.

UTILIZING JOHARI WINDOW FOR TEAM BUILDING

Not just for self-growth, the Johari window can be used to build better teams. Specifically, for the new managers, things are entirely unfamiliar on both sides. Johari's framework offers an opportunity to provide an environment where people can expand their open areas by reducing blind and hidden areas. First-time managers should not hesitate in taking corrective feedback from the peers. Simultaneously, they should make sure they reveal information that can be useful for the team members.

As mentioned, the Johari window has a wide range of applications. However, the fundamental assumptions remain the same, that is, understanding what others think of me. In one of the conversations with an ex-student and a young manager at a steel company, he said, 'One of my team members was up for a leadership role. Unfortunately, people were not comfortable talking with him or discussing their issues and had no trustworthy relationship with him even though he held tremendous knowledge. I feel that image is everything. People tend to treat us based on the way we project ourselves. In this case, since this guy was too career-centric and came across as serious, my colleagues avoided talking to him outside of work. This backfired him as he received a poor rating from his fellow colleagues in a 360-degree performance ratings. His overall rating in the performance appraisal went down and despite being one of the most deserving candidates due to his skillsets, his name was chucked out of the list of prospects.'

SHOULD YOU LISTEN TO EACH AND EVERY FEEDBACK? HOW DO YOU DECIDE WHAT TO CONSIDER SERIOUSLY?

It depends. It depends upon who is offering you the feedback and in what context. For example, if your boss suggests some improvement actions to you, you should take it seriously. If you ask your peers for corrective suggestions, pick and choose the ones that are commonly occurring. And at the same time, come out of the 'I do not care what they say' zone. Note that if one colleague said something about you, you might choose to ignore it because they may not know you enough. If two colleagues said something, it could be a propaganda against you. But if many people said the same thing, it becomes important to understand where it is coming from, what you lack and what is going wrong.

* 8 *

THE BEGINNING

In the previous seven chapters, we explored why self-management, understanding others and managing relationships are important. We also saw why, despite self-awareness being critical, seeking feedback from others and incorporating the corrective suggestions into our lives are equally important. For learning, growth and success of early managers, everything that has been discussed previously in the book remains essentially crucial. However, at a macro level, is there a greater design that operates, or are these just somethings that we as humans made up? In the next section, I intend to provide you with a cosmic perspective, conceived by Dr Neil deGrasse Tyson (Director—Hayden Planetarium), through which I will try to articulate why, despite our seemingly divisive differences, we might want to embrace the fact that we are all one and should actively try to get over our differences.

THE COSMIC PERSPECTIVE

Let me begin by first placing the credit where credit is due for this cosmic perspective.[1] Dr Tyson is known to have

---

[1] https://www.haydenplanetarium.org/tyson/essays/2007-04-the-cosmic-perspective.php

famously said that we are not special because we're different, we're special because we're the same, not just as each other but also as the universe.

Shortly after the universe was formed, the only naturally available atom was hydrogen. These atoms were predominantly found in large gas clouds, which collapsed under their own gravity to form the first stars. At the core of these stars, high pressure and temperature led to the fusion of hydrogen atoms to form helium atoms, which are heavier than hydrogen. These stars then exploded at the end of their lives, in a phenomenon we know as a supernova, and spread the constituents of their core, now enriched with helium, into the cosmos, forming new gas clouds. These new clouds then collapse under their own gravity, again, to form the next generation of stars, in which the high pressure and temperature of the core lead to the formation of elements heavier than helium.

This process repeats over and over and has led to the formation of all the heavier elements in the universe. Every atom present in our bodies is traceable to the crucible known as the core of a star that manufactured these elements and, in death, exploded into a supernova, thus, spreading the enriched contents of its core for the formation of other gas clouds, stars, planets and, at least on one planet, life.

We need to understand that we are all of the SAME lineage. The lineage of stardust. We all came from the dust left over from the explosion of a star that predates our Sun. We are all the 'children' of the same parent, stardust. This bond can never be broken by any known mechanism that operates in our daily lives. Thus, it only makes sense that we set our superficial differences aside and get to know each other better for a more meaningful personal and professional life!

WHAT NEXT?

While it's true that same charges repel and opposite ones attract, the differences among our species are only at the surface. Fundamentally, we all are same; we all are alike. Hence, it's really not the difference among our species that brings them together, it's the similarities that make them huddle with each other. A porcupine always tends to huddle with other porcupines during cold to share heat; it never comes close to, say, a duck! But they end up hurting each other due to their sharp spines. Humans are just like these porcupines. We cannot survive without each other. We need one another for every small and big thing in life. The only challenge is that too big or pokey spines (i.e., our idiosyncrasies) do not let us stay together and create conflicts and differences. Our aim should be to identify those challenging areas, be it the self or others, and minimize their negative effects. Ultimately, we all need to stay together to survive and thrive. And as Aristotle said,

> Man is by nature a social animal; an individual who is unsocial naturally and not accidentally is either beneath our notice or more than human. Society is something that precedes the individual. Anyone who either cannot lead the common life or is so self-sufficient as not to need to, and therefore does not partake of society, is either a beast or a God.

So, take out important learnings from each chapter; see what you need the most at this point. Do not overwhelm yourself with too many changes in yourself or too many commitments. That would dissolve the purpose of self–growth. Start making smaller changes. Give yourself realistic and doable goals. For any habit to come, it takes at least 21 days. Follow this rule in your journey of self-growth too. Nobody is perfect in this world. Nobody knows everything. You achieve in life when you know your weak areas, accept it and embrace it. You promise yourself that you will work on it to become a better person with each passing day. That is what you call an achievement!

ACKNOWLEDGEMENTS

This book will not be complete without thanking my husband, Sanju, who always prioritized my success over his own and wholeheartedly took care of the household chores and our cats, both pets and fosters, during my writing and after. My sincere thanks to my mother for continually pushing me to outshine myself. My love to my sister, who, despite her busy schedules, lent an ear to me to vent out. My gratitude to Professor Debashis Chatterjee, who believed in me and gave me this opportunity to write a piece about something close to my heart and offered me a platform to express my thoughts. Thanks to my student Anju Titus for being kind enough to take out the time to help me by drawing illustrations for this book.

ACKNOWLEDGEMENTS